THE G●LDEN CLIMATE

IN DISTANCE LEARNING

THE SECRETS OF IMMEDIATE CONNECTION, ENGAGEMENT, ENJOYMENT, AND PERFORMANCE

Dr. Marina Kostina & Dr. William LaGanza

MINDSTIR MEDIA

The Golden Climate in Distance Learning

Photography by Naja Lerus (www.najalerusphotography.com)
and Vee Speers (www.veespeers.com)

Cover design by Jill Harron

Published by Mindstir Media
PO Box 1681 | Hampton, New Hampshire 03843 | USA
1.800.767.0531 | www.mindstirmedia.com

Printed in the United States of America

ISBN-13: 978-0-9836771-7-8

Library of Congress Control Number: 2012935448

To Audrey,

William LaGanza

To my family,

Marina Kostina

Ya para entonces me había dado cuenta que buscar era mi signo, emblema de los que salen de noche sin propósito fijo, razón de los matadores de brújulas.

Julio Cortázar, *Rayuela*

["I realized that searching was my symbol, the emblem of those who go out at night with nothing in mind, the motives of a destroyer of compasses."

Julio Cortázar]

CONTENTS

INTRODUCTION

About the book

It's not about acting, it's about interrelating...

Online teaching and training can be one of the most emotional experiences in your professional life — and one that leaves you feeling the most vulnerable. Even seasoned specialists can feel like novices when faced with educating a group at a distance. They are often not sure how to close the cyber gap: how to transfer knowledge and foster learning via computer. If your sense of humor can usually guarantee your success and strong connection with an audience in a face-to-face context, your joke in the online environment is likely to disappear into the abyss, and you can only hope to receive a sign that someone actually found it funny. You spend hours preparing a seminar but you do not see the eyes of your audience and cannot be sure if they really understood the material or enjoyed your presentation.

Some of your students and trainees will disappear into cyberspace without warning, and no amount of e-mails will ever bring them back. The asynchronous communication often feels unnatural and awkward, and the lack of "netiquette" skills often results in unprofessional and unproductive interactions. Even in a synchronous communication your conversation might be left mid-sentence as the minds of your students and trainees get hijacked by some other program, social network site, or smartphone application. While engaging in multitasking in a face-to-face communication is considered poor etiquette, many people have no problem browsing the web, checking their e-mails, or typing text messages during your online presentations, and you can find yourself constantly fighting for their attention.

How can you traverse the cyber landscape and move beyond frustrations to experiencing the joy and the power of this new educational context? How can you transcend your feeling of isolation while simultaneously fostering learner autonomy? How can you increase learner engagement, performance, and retention?

Unfortunately, despite the fact that distance learning has gained enormous popularity in the last decade and only continues to grow, the majority of teachers and trainers do not receive adequate preparation for this environment. They are thrown online and are expected to learn as they go. Many of us understand that being qualified to teach and train does not necessarily mean that we possess those qualities that are effective online, and we often do not have a clue as to what these qualities are and where to get them. Strained for time, we are lost among millions of bits and pieces of information found on the web as the field of distance learning is dominated by fragmented theories and often opposing frameworks. Most publications on distance learning are focused primarily on the technology itself and not the pedagogy. The Internet is full of sites that provide long lists of best practice that travel from one blogger to another and that are often atheoretical in nature.

Therefore, the goal of this book is to offer simple, practical suggestions that can be implemented in any distance learning environment and provide the missing link between theory and practice, connecting technology and pedagogy. We understand that teachers and trainers do not have time in their busy lives to explore various scientific studies dedicated to distance learning. We have done this for you. This book is a result of thorough studies conducted by both authors during many years of university research on distance learning, and years of online teaching, coaching, and training. The core concept, the Golden Climate in Distance Learning™, is based on the Dynamic Interrelational Space model developed by Dr. LaGanza (2001), which revealed how to achieve the optimal teacher-student emotional and intellectual climate that is needed for successful online learning and was confirmed in his later publications (2002, 2004, 2008), as well as by the university research of Dr. Kostina (2011). We are confident that this book will help you realize that the online context is different from that of the traditional classroom, and therefore requires a different pedagogical approach. You will be encouraged to rethink the way you deliver your courses or training seminars at a distance. We seek to ignite your love and appreciation for this educational environment and will demonstrate that distance learning is not only compatible to traditional, face-to-face learning, but in some aspects is superior to it.

Our main objective is to help you find your own online pedagogy, establish your own presence, and build a climate that provides instant and enthusiastic teacher-learner and learner-learner connectivity, and that boosts learner autonomy, engagement, and enjoyment of the learning and teaching processes so that you can succeed in any distance learning setting, with any learning management system (LMS). Our research on student and teacher beliefs and perceptions of distance learning, years of observations of some of the most effective distance learning trainers, and our personal trial and error experiences have resulted in the creation of the Golden Climate in Distance Learning™ method that is revealed in this book. You will discover that in order to establish the Golden Climate, it is not enough to know about distance learning or to learn what to do to be successful. Teachers and trainers must be willing to be a certain way that might redefine traditional understanding of their roles and might push them out of their comfort zone. We all know that "telling is not teaching." Well, doing does not necessarily result in learning, either. The secret is in changing the way we are. We cannot possibly create an online environment that encourages learner autonomy if we are not autonomous ourselves. We cannot build a comfortable atmosphere in our seminars if we ourselves are not comfortable with conducting seminars at a distance. Teachers must be willing to achieve a state of mind/emotion that will help them create a potential space for learning within the teacher-learner relationship — a secure space where the learner can take the risk to be autonomous in their relationship with the teacher and in which the teacher can take the risk of being a facilitator and a resource, encouraging the learner to investigate, discuss, and produce a response to a question in their own way, rather than being a director and telling the learner exactly what to learn and how to learn it. This is the space where both the learner and the teacher can grow: where the learner can learn and the teacher can increase her sensitivity to and understanding of how to make the most of this potential space for learning.

When the teachers are fostering an interrelational climate that is facilitating creativity and enjoyment among the students, they are creating the Golden Climate for that context at that time. Such climates feature friendliness and openness, and acknowledge the importance of helping students to be themselves online. The Golden Climate in Distance Learning™ requires particular cognitive and affective qualities from every member of the learning community in order to develop autonomy and generate knowledge through a social construction of meaning. No other book on distance learning focuses on the interrelational dynamics between the teacher/trainer and the learner despite the fact that this is the very core of the successful interaction online.

Mastering the secrets of this climate will help you conquer the distance from the very first day. Our book will help you to be immediately in control of the distance, and to create YOUR unique Golden Climate with your trainees and students online that is reflective of YOUR teaching and training philosophy, YOUR personality, and YOUR preferred teaching style. We will help you to be the best that you can be — to shine online. In this journey you will be guided through a series of interconnected phases:

1. First, you will be provided with an instant connection toolkit that will allow you to establish successful communication online and to make a positive first impression.

2. Second, you will need to identify, acknowledge, and face your fears. You will be prompted to discover and rewire various patterns and misconceptions regarding distance learning that prevent you from enjoying this educational context. You will learn about the nature of online learning and gain valuable insights into the ways in which you can utilize this environment to benefit your students.

3. Third, you will discover how to use best practice in an effective way to ensure its successful application online.

4. You will realize which cognitive and affective aspects of your being need to be developed in order to cultivate the Golden Climate, an optimal learning environment online.

5. Finally, you will also have access to the Q and A section provided at the end of the book, which is based on the most common questions we have received from our clients and colleagues.

Who is this book for?

This book is designed for online teaching professionals in colleges, universities, and schools; trainers in corporate, professional, and military fields; and other specialists in distance education, training, and communications who want to become more effective online and enjoy this educational context.

How will this book help you?

After reading this book you will be able to

1. find the tools for INSTANT connection with your audience and for establishing a positive atmosphere online from day one;

2. know how to STOP being threatened by the online environment and APPRECIATE its unique features;

3. recognize your most dangerous misconceptions about distance learning and find ways to AVOID them;

4. learn how to create an interrelational climate that BOOSTS learner engagement, collaboration, and autonomy, and SHORTENS the distance online;

5. realize why you NEVER want to limit yourself to general "best practice," and find out how to go BEYOND it in order to create your own ultimate learning environment for your students and trainees;

6. choose THE BEST teaching and training strategies that match YOUR teaching style and personality;

7. grasp THE ART of "in-mind" teaching to provide support and continuously motivate your students;

8. accept that your proven face-to-face strategies might be TOTALLY wrong online, and learn how to find the RIGHT way to transfer your talents at a distance;

9. understand why dealing with discomfort and your personal doubts is not only natural but IMPERATIVE in order to foster learner autonomy;

10. detect various types of interactions that exist online, and use them to MINIMIZE your workload and INCREASE student collaboration and engagement;

11. discover the secrets of the Critical "In-Mind" Boundary that will help you RAISE student autonomy and AVOID student isolation and withdrawal;

12. master the GOLDEN RULES of interrelation that will help you BE an effective online teacher;

13. APPRECIATE the online teaching/learning context as being THE PREFERRED CONTEXT for debating ideas and constructing group and individual projects.

We are positive that creating the Golden Climate in your classroom will enable you to relax and enjoy teaching, and to let the learners enjoy themselves, too. You will know that enjoyment is not a frivolous thing, but necessary to a successful experience. Learners' motivation will come not just from your subject matter, but from the pleasure of working creatively in the climate that you have built with them, as they investigate, discuss, and construct responses to questions or topics that perhaps they have negotiated and established themselves, too.

What this book is NOT

This book is not a training manual on how to develop activities online, or how to choose and use a learning management system. It is not aimed at developing technical skills you might need online.

Before we begin, we would like to introduce you to your virtual guides: a new trainer, Novo, and a seasoned online teacher, Lauri, who will accompany you on your journey.

A note regarding our terminology: For the purposes of this book, the terms online leaning and distance learning are used to refer to a web-based distance learning environment with either synchronous or asynchronous (or both) interaction between the teacher/trainer and a student/trainee.

We also use trainer/teacher and student/trainee interchangeably.

If you have any questions or concerns, if you want to share your success, or if you need any advice, please e-mail us at:
info@goldenclimateindistancelearning.com.

You will usually get a response within forty-eight to seventy-two hours, depending on whether we are traveling or training. We have offered this information for you because we remember how lonely it felt to be new to the online environment. We want to provide you with the opportunity to correspond directly with us, the authors of the book, and to be provided with the answers that are important to you.

CHAPTER 1

NO MORE FEARS:
THINGS YOU NEED TO KNOW

"What we resist, persists"

-Sonia Johnson

Our beliefs about online teaching and training are important to our success in and enjoyment of this environment. If we want to flourish at a distance we must examine our thoughts about this educational context. Often people who dread teaching and training online have pre-programmed fears and misconceptions regarding distance learning that prevent them from being effective and fulfilled online. No matter how much experience or education we have in the "real" world, when it comes to distance learning, the majority of us feel anxiety and frustration. When we start web-based teaching or training for the first time, we hope that this new environment will be similar to the traditional one. We yearn to be able to transfer our skills, talents, and methodologies in this context. We dream of a motivated, responsive, interactive group of learners who will debate intelligently and work independently as producers of ideas. We long for enjoyment, spark, and wit — we want the virtual classroom to come alive, like the face-to-face classroom. However, we quickly learn that the specifics of the new medium require a new set of pedagogical, technical, administrative, and even interpersonal skills. Since most of us do not have any distance learning teacher training before we start our work online, we often begin to feel insecure, intimidated, and even afraid of the distance.

These kinds of negative beliefs paralyze our ability to appreciate and enjoy this educational context. Our worst nightmares regarding distance learning seem to become our reality, as whatever we put our attention on suddenly reveals new unknowns and complexities. How can one be afraid of distance learning and at the same time be an effective trainer or teacher? How can one build a welcoming atmosphere online while resenting this educational environment? The deeper our fears, the fewer the opportunities for fostering learning, and the more of what we do not want comes our way, as "what we resist, persists." Our heads are full of negative messages that start shouting at us way before we even give this new educational context a chance:

"I'm afraid of technology! I'm just not good with it!"

"My students will laugh at me behind their screens!"

"I'll never be able to build connection online. I need to see people."

"I don't know if my trainees enjoyed my presentation. How will I know what they think of it?"

These fears not only limit our capacity for success but are often projected onto our audience. Any emotion is literally "energy in motion." Most trainees are very sensitive to the way their trainers feel and can pick up on their "vibes" from any distance. If the teacher is confident, her confidence is transferred to her students. If the teacher is afraid, the opposite is, unfortunately, also true. Therefore, we are responsible for facing our fears in order to create a peaceful and productive environment, not only for ourselves but also for those whom we train.

Let's examine the fears that you might have developed about distance learning. In the space provided, briefly answer each question:

What are your fears about working online? Write down all fears that come to mind.

_____

_____

_____

_____

_____

Are there any others that are perhaps a bit hard to own up to?

_____

_____

_____

How do you think these fears prevent you from being successful and enjoying the online environment?

_____

_____

_____

_____

_____

How do you think these fears affect your students/ trainees and your communication with them?

_____

_____

_____

_____

_____

Fear is a sign of strain that arises from the conflict between what you want and what you think you can do. Since we often do not understand the online environment, this strain is felt deeply. One of the main functions of our brain is to keep us protected and safe by constantly trying to make sense of everything that we see around us and explain that which we do not understand. In order to feel in control, we need to be able to predict what happens next, since the lack of control brings stress and frustration into our lives. Therefore, if we encounter any information gaps, our mind starts searching for patterns and fills them with its own understanding of reality. In this way, the human brain creates meaning in order to fight ambiguity. Dr. Gazzaniga, professor of psychology and the director for the SAGE Center for the Study of the Mind at the University of California Santa Barbara, studied people who had undergone split-brain surgery. In these patients, whose left and right brain hemispheres do not communicate with each other, the brain always tries to develop a complete picture and fill in the perceived information voids. When the patients were shown different pictures — some pictures to one brain hemisphere, some to the other — the patients' interpretation of the "missing" information was not based on reality, but solely on their own imagination.

Therefore, our minds are wired to neglect, diminish, or provide explanations for things that we do not understand. When we do not have enough information about distance learning, we start justifying our frustrations with negative thoughts about this context. As a result we grow bitter and unappreciative, and stop believing in the power of this educational environment. The newly developed negative image captivates our brain and stirs our emotions. Whatever we focus on online seems more and more to merit our rejection, so the death spiral continues. The online environment degenerates into a cyber jungle full of fatal traps: the more negativity we have, the less chance we have to survive there — and to enjoy it. We frantically search the Internet, trying to find the cure for our fears. We apply "best strategies" that will make it all okay. However, until we understand the nature of this unique environment and gain knowledge that will help us calm our fears and take account of the misconceptions that our brain has created in its attempts to protect us from the unknown, we will never be able to succeed with such strategies.

Both success and fears come from our thoughts. You have the capacity to choose your thoughts and rewire your perceptions of distance learning. The first step towards effective online teaching and training is to get to KNOW this educational environment. An old Irish saying states: "Fear knocked at the door, knowledge answered, and no one was there." Once you gain enough knowledge about online learning, you will see your fears start to disappear. Your mind will start searching for the tools that can help you deal with this reality, and you will first move into the zone of "doing" and then into the realm of "being," which will be explored in detail in the next chapters.

Let's now "open the door" to our fears and discuss how they shape our understanding or, better, misunderstanding of the reality online. Below we have compiled some common fears and associated misconceptions that are shared by many teachers and trainers. We have then provided research-based descriptions of distance learning that will hopefully change your misconceptions and show you the "true" nature of distance learning. In particular, we have tried to show you how these feelings can prevent you from moving toward an appreciation and enjoyment of this environment. Like most fears and misconceptions, there's a grain of truth in each of them; but being able to discern fact from fiction is a good first step toward feeling more confident in the online environment and appreciating its potential for your students and trainees.

The fears that we discuss below are as follows:

1. Fear of communicating online
2. Fear of silence
3. Fear of technology
4. Fear of managing online courses
5. Fear of looking foolish and incompetent

FEAR #1: Fear of Communicating Online

Many teachers and trainers admit that they are afraid to communicate online. They believe that they are more prone to being unclear and misunderstood in this environment because the majority of communication occurs through written interactions. Most of them are accustomed to using spoken words in the classroom that are accompanied by their body language and facial expressions. Written communication, on the contrary, is deprived of clues. Therefore, it takes much more effort for a teacher or a trainer to be understood correctly in this educational setting and to provide her students with sufficient information. In addition, many trainers report that they are afraid to handle discussions at a distance. Setting up chats, forums, and any other collaborative activities is already a big challenge for many, but making sure that they are used effectively is an even bigger responsibility. Most teachers are not sure of their own role in this process and therefore often give up incorporating any collaborative elements into their classroom. This makes them feel "safer," but it also minimizes the full capacity of Learning Management Systems (LMSs) and limits them to being used solely as content holders.

Misconception: *Distance Learning is impersonal and cold.*

Fear of online communication often forms a view of distance learning as an impersonal and cold environment. Certainly, despite its numerous benefits, web-based distance learning is far from being an optimal educational context. While high-tech developments bring attractive and glamorous features to the distance learning environment, these very same technological advancements have been criticized for dehumanizing the educational process, and have posed several challenges that are specific to this new learning context. Many teachers and trainers complain that distance learning is deprived of physical interactions and therefore is emotion-less. Their logic is as follows: since the online environment does not support physical interactions such as eye contact, gestures, and facial expressions through which relationships are built in a face-to-face environment, then by default distance learning is not capable of facilitating true connections. However, these teachers might not have contemplated the fact that connections online can be developed in a different way from those formed face-to-face.

Research-Based "Reality"

Research shows that not only the online environment but also traditional classrooms can feel distant to students and trainees. The result is a lack of engagement and interest in participating in meaningful interactions with other members of the learning environment (Moore, 1993, 2007; Saba, 2000; Stirling, 1997). For example, according to Moore's Transactional Distance Theory (1993), transactional distance can be a part of any educational context. It is a distance of understanding and connection between a teacher and a student, a "psychological space or communications gap between students and teachers that must be negotiated in order to maximize learning" (Burgess, 2006). This theory assumes that the most profound impact on online education is pedagogy and not the physical or temporal distance that separates teacher and learner. With the right pedagogy that is tailored to distance learning and effective student-teacher dialogue strategies, transactional distance can be minimized.

Although the relational points of reference between trainers and trainees change from the classroom to the online context, this does not necessarily mean that in distance learning there is a "lack" of connection. On the contrary, research shows that communication between a teacher and a student who might never physically meet each other can be even more intimate and extensive online (Revenaugh, 2000; Perreault, et. al., 2002). Since the role of the successful teacher online is no longer one of an "expert who knows it all" (we will discuss this role in more detail later in the book), her communication with her students becomes more personal. Teachers become active participants in the learning community, who guide, discuss, encourage, and offer resources, and therefore are more approachable and less intimidating to their students. This transformation of the teacher's role enhances not only mentor-mentee relationships, but also those among the students (Kemp, 2000).

Due to the ongoing nature of the distance learning course and its availability 24/7 in comparison to the periodic nature of a face-to-face course that meets on a certain day for a certain time, there is more space for interaction, for developing a thought in-depth: before expressing it, and for offering or seeking support online. Moreover, the majority of online courses are asynchronous, i.e., not all members of the learning community are online at the same time. This feature of distance learning brings more freedom to students and trainees in their responses to their classmates. Their interactions tend to be more honest and open due to some degree of anonymity that is provided by the online environment (Wood, 2005). It allows students and trainees to speak up and provides emotional comfort (Kindred, 2000). Emotional safety is so important for students that it often can compensate for the occasional technical frustrations experienced online. Because distance learning creates fewer opportunities for being put on the spot, many introverted students flourish in this educational context and even choose it over the traditional one (Burnett, 2001; Bolliger & Martindale, 2004; Warschauer, 1998). For example, one of our research participants stated:

> There is more stress in a face-to-face classroom…there is more you can see…when the teacher calls on you or wants you to say something and you mess up. It is embarrassing because you are physically in the classroom and all students know who you are, but in the online classroom it does not feel as stressful, it is more anonymous as you are not actually there physically. I like to work on my own when I feel anxiety and to be able to connect with others when I feel like socializing.

Introverted students are not the only ones who prefer working solo online. Extroverts also seem to enjoy web-based interactions (Daughenbaugh & Ensminger, 2003; Kelly & Schorger, 2002). Some participants of our study, who were extroverted college students and world travelers, also liked to be "left alone" online. One of them confessed:

> I feel a little bit [of] isolation [online], but I like it. I don't need to worry about other people looking at my facial expression when I don't know something as I have some awkward feeling. I don't need to talk to anyone or explain something to my peers if they don't understand it. I always do work ahead of time so I don't fall behind and I like that I can do it on my own, without waiting until the whole class gets it to proceed to a new topic.

In addition, the distance learning context allows students to explore resources that they would otherwise not be able to access in a traditional classroom (Revenaugh, 2000). Online students can find various types of media at a click of the mouse, and match their learning styles with the corresponding information medium. The availability of these materials and abundance of extra resources can provide more access to knowledge online than in a face-to-face environment. Hence it is important to teach online students to think critically about the plausibility of information they find on the web: while browsing articles, they need to maintain a critical intellectual attitude concerning how arguments are constructed (logical, consistent, valid?) and the quality of sources (peer-reviewed in scholarly journals and books). The aim of a critical intellectual attitude is to look at what the author argues, why, and how; how the argument is supported; and whether, on this basis, the argument is plausible.

To conclude, distance learning is not inherently impersonal. Your students and trainees can feel disconnected even in traditional classes. Our research demonstrates that distance learning has a potential for building even deeper connections and closer relationships than face-to-face, provided you use strategies that are designed specifically for this educational context. In the next chapter we will show you what to DO to make your online training and teaching very personal and promote communication among all members of the learning community. For now we would just like you to put aside your fears, dissolve your misconceptions, and give this exciting educational environment a try.

FEAR# 2: Fear of Silence

Many teachers and trainers admit that they are afraid of the silence online. If in a face-to-face context they know how to spot struggling students or trainees, online they are unaware of whether their students experience alienation, frustration, anxiety, anger, loneliness, or boredom. Silence is expressed in the same way by those who are autonomous and successful, and those who need help. Teachers and trainers who are used to being able to pick up on students' facial expressions of confusion or unhappiness and take appropriate measures to ensure that students understand the material do not have that luxury online (White, 2000).

Misconception: *Online courses aren't as good as face-to-face courses.*

The hallmark of this teacher's fear is staggering, terrifying silence that penetrates the entire cyberspace between the trainer and the trainee. For some mentors, silence means indifference; for others, it is a sign of cynicism and hostility. It can also be a sign of students' shyness, reticence, or even withdrawal from the course. However, few teachers and trainers are aware that student silence can also be born of students' reacting to the teacher's own fears that they project online — a silence that only increases teacher anxiety. In order to avoid feeling vulnerable, teachers create another misconception about distance learning: that the online environment is not as good as the traditional one.

Research-Based "Reality"

Research shows over and over that it is largely pedagogy that makes teaching effective or ineffective, not the medium of teaching itself. A substantial body of research on distance learning from 1952 to 1992 demonstrated that both distance learning and the traditional classroom environment provided similar outcomes (DeSantis, 2002; Phipps & Merisotis, 1999). Russell (2001) also analyzed numerous studies and provided support for the "no significant difference" phenomenon. Besides, there is a number of benefits of distance learning over the traditional environment. For instance, the distance learning student's ability to take control of his learning online is connected with his satisfaction (Benson, 2001; Dickinson, 1995; Holec, 1979). One of our study participants, Anne, stated that the online environment helped her to stay focused and not to fall behind. She said, "I like that the materials are there for you. You can always go back and repeat all information that you missed or to repeat it before the test." Another student, Jake, also confirmed that control of learning was related to his satisfaction with distance learning. He said:

> It [online learning] is less on the professor and more on the student.... The professor cannot be there for you unless if you ask for her help.... So you need to do your assignment, send it to her and get your grade. You don't need to depend on the teacher. You choose what to do when you have an issue.

Therefore, being in control of one's learning environment is an important feature of distance education. It allows students to understand that learning does not just happen to them but that they are active participants in the learning process.

Another feature of distance learning that is strongly related to student satisfaction is the ability to make their own decisions (Holec. 1979, Benson, 2001, White, 2006). For instance, our study participant, Alex, enjoyed the opportunity to decide when to study and to schedule his week according to his priorities:

I like the ability to self-pace online. I can just take one day and do all of my homework if I want to. Sometimes I have a deadline at work and I cannot study at all during that time. But then, after the deadline I can put in sixteen hours if I need to into my class. So I like how you can do it when you want to and put in as much as you want to into it.

In addition, despite the fact that many teachers and trainers might find it counter-intuitive, research shows that experiencing a certain degree of isolation online seems to be desirable for many students. Many online participants prefer to work alone, which suggests, according to Little (1991), a "capacity for detachment." In the following chapters we will show you how you can work with the student need for autonomy to enhance the educational experience, without pushing him into the isolation and withdrawal zone. For now we would like you to open up your mind to this new educational environment and accept that its unique qualities can be useful for your trainees and students.

FEAR #3: Fear of Technology

Many trainers express anxiety and even panic when it comes to technology. They believe that they will always be perceived as digital emigrants (Prensky, 2001), and will never be able to catch up with the tech-savvy digital natives who happen to be their students and trainees. It is understandable that it might feel uncomfortable for the teachers who used to be the experts and the gurus in the classroom to realize that they are less competent in this area that their mentees. Teachers and trainers often feel unsure of how they will give knowledge to the generation that does not read books but that was "born" with the computer in their hands. However, teachers need to realize that the idea of "giving knowledge" comes from the modernist approach where knowledge transfer was the goal of teaching. In order to teach successfully online, the new generation of teachers who remotely connect with their students will not only have to learn how to use different technologies, they will have to develop a whole new set of assumptions about what teaching is and how it works. Postmodern technologies need postmodern teaching, where the teacher acts as a negotiator of meaning, a resource, a facilitator in the process of the students' producing knowledge, rather than as a "knowledge transfer" teacher forcing the consumption of ideas and colonizing the learner's mind with her own world view.

The problem for modernist or traditional teachers is not just learning new technology: it is learning new technology and new pedagogy combined. This is a large contributor to their fear: they sense, or they know, that not only is their technical knowledge obsolete, but their pedagogical knowledge, as well. The difficult thing for them to realize is that the way they have been teaching all their lives will greatly limit their students' learning and development online — just as it does in the classroom — but in the classroom they can get away with knowledge transfer because in a face-to-face context, where the institution and the teacher form a powerful presence, there is no learner anonymity and it is more difficult, politically and emotionally, for a student to drop out.

These teachers can't envisage transferring their teaching from the classroom to online, because their assumptions about how learning works are not adapted to the new technology. They need a shift from the right answer to the validly argued perspective, from the exercise to the project, from authority to facilitating the learners' investigation of a topic and the generation of a well-argued and supported point of view with which they might not agree. They need a shift from being the controller to creating with their learners the interrelational conditions in which a learner's autonomy can develop and in which the learner can bloom: the Golden Climate.

Misconception: *My classes/training sessions cannot be converted to distance learning.*

Because teachers and trainers feel intimidated by technology, their minds start to function as defense mechanisms, creating rationalizations for opting out. They admit that distance learning might be useful for some classes but that THEIR classes cannot be successfully transferred online. We hear all the time from both trainers and teachers that they believe in the overall power of distance learning, but that they cannot imagine their topic being converted to distance learning. Interestingly, such statements come from the trainers and teachers from various fields, even those in which others have successfully created distance learning programs for their specific topics.

Research-Based "Reality"

We agree there are some aspects of technology that can be frustrating. For example, research shows that inevitable technical glitches and slow Internet connections may seriously impair learning and even be one of a number of reasons for student dissatisfaction with a course, resulting in students' withdrawal. These barriers can also create the potential for misunderstandings between students and teachers and increase student isolation online. It can also be more difficult to train in a subject that requires in-person performances, or needs immediate feedback (such as foreign language studies or nursing). However, there are numerous ways to overcome these obstacles in the modern distance learning context. Not all distance learning courses and training sessions should be developed asynchronously (i.e. purely online). The use of a hybrid course that involves online and face-to-face formats becomes preferable in certain situations. Today's technological development allows face-to-face components to also be used online through various web conferencing systems, such as WebX, Wimba, and Elluminate, and countless desktop applications, such as GotoMeetings and Microsoft NetMeeting.

Certainly, in order to teach and train at a distance one needs some time to learn new programs. The real fear of technology started a long time ago, when online learning involved engaging with not very user-friendly software and often required teachers to know more about technology than they really needed to know. Nowadays, learning management systems are much more user-orientated. Many teachers and trainers are fluent with the Internet and even have their own social network connections and affiliations. When it comes to technical knowledge, studies show that teachers and trainers do not need to be experts in online technologies in order to create effective training and teaching at a distance. Students are happy to use their own ability to navigate cyberspace using their high-tech powers and following the guidance of their teachers and trainers. In the next chapter we will show how to draw upon your students' advanced technological knowledge without having to become tech gurus yourselves. For the time being, we just want you to take your focus off technology and consider changing your role as a leader in every aspect of the educational experience, through giving your students more power over the learning process and supporting them as they use it. You are still in charge, as the "e" in any type of e-learning should really stand for context-appropriate education, not technology.

FEAR # 4: Fear of Managing Online Courses

Even the most seasoned online trainers and educators at times cannot overcome their fear of managing online courses. Because online courses require a different type of preparation, organization, and feedback system, approaching this environment with the same tools that are used in face-to-face settings almost always guarantees failure and dismay. We see numerous brilliant teachers and trainers enduring intolerable stress trying to correct mountains of papers and answering e-mails that seem to come in non-stop. It is thus understandable why many professionals are terrified of working in this environment, despite its flexibility and convenience.

Misconception: *Distance learning is much more time-consuming than traditional learning.*

The fear of managing distance learning gives birth to a common misconception: that distance learning requires much more time and effort than traditional classes. Many teachers complain that they are "buried" online and do not have any time for their professional growth, social, and personal lives. Not seeing how to get out of the cycle of correcting papers and answering e-mails, they associate distance learning with an enormous workload.

Research-Based "Reality"

Research demonstrates that traditional strategies of teaching and training do not necessarily work online. They can make distance learning overwhelming and time-consuming for both mentors and mentees. On the other hand, research also indicates that some of the most effective activities online are more project- and activity-based, where the traditional role of teacher and students has been redesigned. Certainly, it still takes considerable time to develop such activities, but once they are built they can be reused and accommodated to different contexts, and in the long run are more fun and successful for the learners. Learners have increased enjoyment, motivation, and performance with these kinds of activities, because learners can initiate and build up pieces of work that correspond to their interests. At the same time, they develop higher-level, deep-learning thinking skills, such as those required to find appropriate information, to develop a point of view, to argue the plausibility of ideas in discussions with colleagues, or to compare and contrast different perspectives. We will discuss distance learning activity- and project-based teaching in more detail later on in this book.

There are also some aspects of distance learning that require less time and effort than face-to-face ones. Working remotely saves you many hours of commute and allows you to teach and train comfortably from your very own home. Another convenient feature of online training is that you can use the administrative features of the LMS to grade, track, and provide feedback with more ease than in a face-to-face classroom. All of your deadlines are posted online and all materials are available to your trainees at any moment. You can check the activity logs of your students to see if they are spending enough time participating in the course and to provide early intervention for those who aren't.

In the next chapter, we will provide you with some concrete strategies that will help you minimize your time in a distance learning course, while at the same time creating a more effective learning experience for the learners. We will also show you how to strategically plan your schedule to accommodate various time demands that are peculiar to distance learning and that will secure the organic flow of your training. For now, we hope that you will start contemplating the idea that distance learning might not be so overburdening as you previously thought and might be more exciting than you originally thought it would be.

FEAR #5: Fear of Looking Foolish and Incompetent

Like their mentees, trainers and teachers often feel under the spotlight online. In a face-to-face environment, they can reveal things about themselves and open up about issues they care about in a spontaneous conversation, without feeling overly exposed; online, all private thoughts and feelings are even more "public." They are literally published on the site or typed into the e-mail messages and forums, and are there to stay. The ability of an LMS to record instantly and permanently our thoughts and emotions gives rise to feelings of enduring vulnerability and exposure to the world, which in turn makes many trainers and teachers feel unsafe and unprotected online. In this environment, they are more afraid of being judged and looking foolish in front of their trainees than in a classroom. A simple phrase or a joke can be taken out of context in a web-based setting. A small grammatical mistake can be associated with incompetence and unprofessionalism and "stare" at everyone for eternity. It is therefore natural for many teachers and trainers to revert to safer practices, limiting themselves to a bare minimum of communication and avoiding the risks associated with opening up and expressing themselves the way they would face-to-face.

Misconception: *Distance learning is a threatening and often "dangerous" environment.*

Standing in front of a group of students in a classroom can be intimidating. However, being in front of the computer screen with many students behind it is even more nerve-wracking. Because many trainers and teachers are afraid to lose face online and be ridiculed by their students, who can easily hide in cyberspace, they might resort to playing safe and avoid taking risks. In 2010, for example, some Australian university lecturers refused to post their pre-recorded lectures online because they were afraid to become victims of students' mockery. Despite the fact that most professors agreed that availability of online materials would be of tremendous help to their students, preservation of their public image was a much stronger motivation factor. Besides their fear that their speech would be ripped apart to become the center of jokes, they were also afraid that their intellectual property would be accessible to outsiders and that their casual phrases and jokes could be taken out of context and misinterpreted.

Research-Based "Reality"

Studies show that students are as much afraid of being ridiculed as their mentors. Many participants in our research talked about their fears of being laughed at by their classmates who can "hide" online and can easily make fun of their mistakes. Students' propensity to feel vulnerable online means that they appreciate a strong and reassuring relationship with their teacher. Their ability to develop a rapport with their mentor is closely related to their overall satisfaction with the online course (Herring & Smaldino, 1997; Lim and Cheah, 2003; Simonson & Russo-Converso, 2001).

The teacher's showing respect for her students also seems to be important for student satisfaction with the teacher and the course (La Ganza, 2001, 2004). Our study participants addressed the theme of respect and agreed that it is an important quality of a good teacher. Students need to feel respected in order to feel good online and to give respect back to their teachers. Therefore, students and trainees feel just as vulnerable online as their mentors. In the following chapter, we will discuss various strategies based on trust and mutual respect that can help you to establish a welcoming and safe environment in your online session. For now, we would like to encourage you to be risk takers and fearlessly explore this educational context.

Now that we have discussed our most common fears and associated misconceptions, let's rewire our brains to a more positive image of distance learning.

In the space provided, please write down all the benefits of distance learning that you can think of:

_____

_____

_____

_____

_____

Now discuss how distance learning will help you as a teacher (trainer):

_____

_____

_____

We hope that after reading this chapter you have gained some useful knowledge about distance learning and can see that it is very different from face-to-face learning. We would like you to start entertaining the idea that online teaching has to be constructivist and not positivist in order to be successful. Modernist/positivist or objectivist teaching is about filling the learner up with objective, indisputable knowledge, as if the learner were a bucket and the teacher were the fountain of knowledge. When the bucket is full, the learning has been acquired. This kind of teaching develops exercises with "right" answers about the way the world objectively is: when the learner has learned all the right answers, according to the teacher's chosen focus, the reality has been acquired.

If, on the contrary, we believe that concepts are constructed and that learning needs to be informed by our students' interests, then we can support them in putting together a piece of work based on perspectives from a variety of sources. This approach helps them gain a nuanced sensitivity to and understanding of the world according to their needs and interests. This is called constructivist or postmodern teaching, which consists of supporting trainees and students in initiating and developing projects. In constructivist/poststructuralist/postmodernist teaching, the teacher, who is a resource and negotiator of meaning, goes on a journey of investigation with the learner as a piece of work is developed — and learns things along the way, sharing in the joys of discovery and the development of ideas. On the other hand, in positivist teaching, the teacher is an authority who knows the right answers, and the learner learns what the teacher tells him to learn. It is difficult for a person who assumes to know an objective reality to problematize the way they think things are — to move from the exercise to the project, from asserting control to fostering autonomy, from teaching facts to generating and validating perspectives in response to questions of interest to the learner. We will discuss the ways to reach such a shift in your pedagogy in the next chapter.

The first step is to get over the misconceptions described in this chapter and any other pre-set views of this environment by understanding how many of them are not actually based on "reality." This knowledge will help dissolve any fears that might hold you back. Now that you have confronted your underlying fears and misconceptions that might hold you back from enjoying and using effectively the online context for your teaching and training purposes, we will discuss the actions that you might want to take. We act upon our thoughts, so put your new awareness into practice to create habits that will allow you to succeed online and enjoy this unique environment. The next section will reveal secrets of successful actions online and will go beyond best practice. It will not only provide a description of the most effective strategies, but will also explain how to use them to create winning training seminars and distance learning classrooms. We are not saying that the journey from fear to success is covered with rose petals. We know it is a difficult one, but we also know that it is totally worth it!

Experts Talk

In order to provide you with more information about distance learning, we conducted in-depth interviews with three leading researchers in the field of distance learning: Dr. Saba, Dr. Gibbs, and Dr. Germain-Rutherford. We hope that these interviews will help you understand this environment better and will answer some questions that you might have about this educational context.

Interview with Dr. Farhad Saba
Professor Emeritus of Educational Technology
San Diego State University, USA

Dr. Saba is professor Emeritus of Educational Technology at San Diego State University (1984 — present), where he teaches courses on distance education. He has been involved in the field of distance education since 1973, first as the managing director of Educational Radio and Television of Iran (1973 —1978), and then as the director of the Telecommunications Division at the University of Connecticut (1979 — 1984).

Dr. Saba has authored more than one hundred articles and chapters in books. He has the distinct honor to be the first winner of the Charles A. Wedemeyer award given to scholars who have made significant contributions to research and theory building in the field of distance education. Dr. Saba has presented in professional conferences in many countries, including Afghanistan, the People's Republic of China, Great Britain, France, Malaysia, Mexico, Sweden, Switzerland (the United Nations), and Turkey. He is on the editorial board of the American Journal of Distance Education, the International Review of Distance and Open Learning, MERLOT's Journal of Online Learning and Teaching, Asia Pacific Education Review, and the Turkish Online Journal of Distance Education.

fsaba@mail.sdsu.edu   www.distance-educator.com

What are some of the main differences in pedagogy between the face-to-face and distance learning contexts?

Distance education is entering the era of post-industrialization as new technologies that make learning at a distance personalized are emerging. These new technologies use a variety of software applications as common as a recommendation engine or as elaborate as artificial intelligence to provide differential responses to learners, based on their prior knowledge, motivation, and aptitude.

Face-to-face education (teaching and learning) is a craft-oriented pre-industrial process that perhaps was personalized at the early stages of its development in higher education and K—12 schools in the late 1800s. However, during the twentieth century, as demand for education increased and mass industrial education took shape, face-to-face education only became possible through an industrial management system in almost all institutions. Highly standardized by nature, a one-size-fits-all management system, therefore, is at odds with the craft-oriented style of teaching and learning in most face-to-face institutions. The inflexibility of the industrial model of educational management in face-to-face institutions has resulted in their decreasing ability to meet the demands of learners, employers, and other stakeholders in a post-industrial society that craves flexibility, personalization, and respect for thinking differently. This inflexibility is also a direct response to a steady increase in the cost of education, three times the rate of inflation in the past three decades.

What is the role of students' and teachers' emotions in the distance learning classroom?

Distance learning literature, directly or indirectly, has dealt with the affective domain in terms of "social presence," "locus of control," or "motivation." The myth is that there is an affective bond between the learner and the teacher in a brick-and-mortar classroom. That, however, depends on the size of the class. In a lecture hall with two hundred learners, the instructor has less social presence than in a class of twenty-five in a distance learning setting. Those who have taught at a distance know that they usually get to know their learners better than in a large face-to-face lecture hall.

How can a teacher promote student autonomy while at the same time prevent students from withdrawing from the class?

Learners have different desires and levels of tolerance for autonomy. Similar to evaluating their prior learning, motivation, and other similar traits, instructors can evaluate a learner's tolerance for autonomy and structure. In the future, instructors will be receiving tremendous help from the next-generation learning management systems (LMS). These dynamic LMSs are bound to be highly interactive and more responsive to a learner's profile. The key, however, for the instructor is to learn as much as possible about the profile of the learner and respond to the learner's traits on an individual basis.

What are some strategies that can be used to encourage student engagement online?

The key factor is to teach learners how to learn, to become aware of his/her metacognitive abilities, emotional intelligence, and behavioral adaptability. Many learners have acquired habits in a teacher-centered model of learning in an educational culture that is still based on a twentieth-century system of industrial education, a system in which the institution or the instructor is supposed to be responsible for the learner's learning. In learning via the Internet the learner is in the driver's seat. It may, however, take one or two generations for all learners to realize that learning has always been a personal task, since teachers in most K—12 schools continue to follow a teacher/institution-centered model of education. In the next two decades, however, learners will be increasingly engaged in what they want to learn in the Internet-based environment, which is an open system and not subject to a standardized regime of education.

How do you know that all is working well in your online classroom?

The bottom line in any educational system is for learners to demonstrate their ability in learning outcomes that are defined for them by an instructor or an instructional system (structure) and learning goals that they have defined for themselves (autonomy). We are good at testing for objectives-based learning outcomes. However, what we need to do is develop predictors that can indicate the potential(s) of the emergent behavioral, cognitive, affective, and experiential states of learners as well as the value of a learner's experiential (phenomenological) learning.

What do you think is the future of distance learning?

What we know is that the number of distance learners has increased on a steady basis since the US Department of Education has collected statistics on learning at a distance. However, one of the basic promises of distance education — that of decreasing the cost of education — has not materialized yet, since most educational institutions are still engaged in a one-size-fits-all model of teaching and learning, albeit they may use the Internet. If the learner's experience is not based on receiving differential treatment based on his/her traits, it really does not matter if s/he is a few inches away from the instructor or thousands of miles away. The key for the future of distance education is to understand that the level of distance in education — or transactional distance — is determined by the rate of autonomy, in a dynamic relation with the rate of structure for each individual learner at each moment in time regardless of the physical distance between the learner and the instructor.

Would you like to add anything else?

I have been involved in the field of distance education for the past thirty five years and have seen it grow and develop from a peripheral activity to a main endeavor. However, I do not think the true promise of distance education has been realized yet. I hope more graduate students decide to learn about the history, theories, and principles of distance education and become practitioners in the field. I particularly emphasize learning about the history of the field, because many practitioners who have joined the field in the past ten or twenty years are unaware of the origins and theoretical developments of the field. This has resulted in many institutions not taking advantage of what distance education affords, and limiting it to twentieth century industrial practice of education in an increasingly post-industrial age. In short, just because it is on the Internet it does not make it distance education.

Interview with Dr. Gibbs
Associate Professor, School of Education
Macquarie University, Sydney, Australia

Dr. Donna Gibbs is an educator who has worked as an English teacher in schools, as an inspector for the N.S.W. Board of Studies, and as an associate professor at Macquarie University, Sydney, Australia. Her publications are on topics as diverse as Elizabethan love poetry, children's literature, film, and cyberculture.

What are some of the main differences in pedagogy between the face-to-face and distance learning contexts?

Good pedagogy, in my view, involves giving access to knowledge and skills in ways that build confidence in the student to use and experiment with them. Doing this face-to-face or online may involve different ways of relating to a student or a group of students, but the goal isn't really different. And even though the ways are physically different, again they are the same. Responding to others in ways that show recognition of their individual qualities is an important part of this.

What is the role of the student's and teacher's emotions in the distance learning classroom?

In a face-to-face environment, as a teacher you can see the expressions and body language of a student for a given period of time, which allows you to respond to their anxieties/pleasures, etc., and accordingly shape how learning ideas are presented to them. This can create a personal bond either related or unrelated to what is being studied/ taught and can have an impact on a student's motivation to learn.

Motivating a student in distance mode involves including personal responses to what they have to say and how they feel about things. Creating an atmosphere and opportunities that encourage students to interact with each other as well as with you is also important. There are more places for people to hide themselves online so you have to be vigilant about ensuring there is "real" contact. Online teaching involves different kinds of judgments about what is happening to students, and about what they know and what they need to know to move more deeply into their learning. A personal contact of whatever sort is an essential part of a teaching role.

How can a teacher promote learner autonomy while at the same time prevent students from withdrawing from the class?

There will always be dropouts for personal reasons, but there are also dropouts that can be prevented by good teaching strategies. These include early assessment of a positive kind if at all possible to indicate concern about their learning and recognition of their strengths and difficulties;

including room for their making choices that suit their own personality/workplace needs/learning ambitions; including some communication that is friendly and fun so being online is a place where you feel accepted and where you are likely to enjoy what you are doing; including a variety of tasks; giving opportunities for those with strengths in a particular area to take a leadership role for a time and share their expertise with others.

What are some strategies that can be used to encourage student engagement online?

Most of the above — personal connection established that is accepting, reasonably broad minded, and warm. I remember Bill's getting students to write about the room where they worked as a starter was a brilliant way to get students engaged. I've never thought of a better one.

How do you know that all is working well in your online classroom?

I guess you never really do, as is the case in any classroom. But good signs are passions and enthusiasms being exchanged; people willing to detour for a bit when something gets interesting; assignments coming in fairly regularly; the quality of the exchanges in discussion; the evidence of students having themselves engaged with the literature; signs of inquiring minds in the discussions; responsiveness between the students themselves to each other's needs; a willingness to give helpful info to each other; a willingness to confide in the teacher about problems they are having, knowing that confidences will not be shared with others.

Interview with Professor Aline Germain-Rutherford,
Associate Vice President for Language Schools.
and Director of the French School
Middlebury College, Vermont, USA

Dr. Germain-Rutherford has authored numerous publications on faculty development, second language pedagogy, speech technology, and the integration of sound pedagogy in e-learning practices. She has headed several national and international research projects, specifically on faculty development and multicultural issues in post-secondary education and online environments. She has been a visiting professor and keynote speaker in Europe, North America, Asia, Africa, and the Middle East. Dr. Germain-Rutherford is also the recipient of the 3M National Teaching Fellow Award, a national Canadian award for excellence in teaching and leadership in higher education.

You have been involved in the development of an online language learning program for students in high schools in the United States. How can we increase student engagement online? You mentioned that a student's documenting their learning experience can help.

The student needs to reflect on how he is doing, to reflect on the activity he is accomplishing and how he is performing. What did he learn from others while interacting with the online materials and his peers — the discovery of a new culture, new ideas? How does it compare to his own culture? All of these questions help him to become more aware of who he is. If I am more aware of who I am, if I'm more aware of the richness of what I'm gaining, more and more, my level of stress is going down because I'm getting more used to what I'm doing.

Your students interact with many different multimedia materials. You seem to combine project development with social interaction, including negotiation, debate, and collaboration.

What we have developed is for high-school students and it is mostly task-based. Our vision is to create a language-learning environment that includes three interrelated, interactive and inter-referential components which, while stimulating each other, can also function autonomously: a core course, and a 3D immersive environment and a virtual collaborative space for students to perform a diversity of tasks while interacting with peers and native speakers. We are still in the process of developing this virtual collaborative space, however presently, to realize projects online students can use different online tools such as comic creator software or VoiceThread (http://voicethread.com/), that are very easy to use, and where students can mix images, audio recordings and/or video recordings, to create and share multimedia projects. Our extensive use of authentic videos filmed across the world and of a diversity of texts allows for students to explore this media rich collection of online resources, to select the relevant information for their project — while developing their listening and reading skills and their cultural awareness. Students meet regularly online with an online instructor on a platform allowing for synchronous interaction to share the information they collected for their project, negotiate and debate what is the most relevant information for their project. Using VoiceThread they can comment on each other's project via text, video, audio communication, they can peer or self-assess their projects. The collaboration allows them to re-use in an authentic communication lots of language structures they learned in the course.

On the basis of their group work, their comments on their own contribution to a project, and their performance on activities, you arrive at an individual assessment in this particular course?

The assessment is an individual assessment because this is what most high school demands. However we have adopted a multifaceted approach to assessment, which includes self-reflective diagnosis, self-graded activities using activity specific rubrics, computer feedback in the form of right/wrong type of feedback, check marks, Teacher graded activities for oral assignments and written assignments, authentic assessment that occurs during online conversation with the teacher and/ or other students durng the collaboration, summative assessment through unit tests.

You have been showing your teachers how to move beyond the traditional step-by-step structural approach in their teaching, working with students to develop challenging learning situations and helping students to be reflexive, accurately self-assess, and be more self-directed on an autonomous basis?

Training the teachers to understand and own this approach is the most difficult and essential part of our work. Language teachers have been trained for many decade in a certain way, they have a certain representation of what learning a language is, and many assumptions about what can and cannot be accomplished in an online environment. I'm talking about Canada and the United States, and it's different in different countries. For many teachers, learning a language still means that you primarily have to focus on structures, and that you start at the level of the word. Working with authentic materials even with beginners is often rejected, by fear that the students who is beginning in the language will not understand. We have therefore to change their perception of what learning a language can be. We have to pull down the resistance that they show. Another point of resistant is the active role a student can play in monitoring his own learning. It is still very difficult for many teachers to see themselves as facilitators, and not as the single knowledge provider. I like to quote this definition I hear once at a conference: "a teacher is a designer of learning situations". All the self and peer assessment activities that we have designed in these online courses, all the self-reflective diagnosis and rubrics that we offer at regular moments within the online courses, help the learner to progressively take charge of his learning. This is often hard for a teacher to accept that a student who is well-guided can progressively accurately assess and reflect on what he can and what he cannot do. The professional development modules that we have created to train the teachers are helping them to realize that the students can be guided to become more autonomous, that they can become develop metacognitive skills to reflect on their learning style and strategies. We are also helping the teacher to become more reflexive himself, to be able to question what he is doing. This is what we are discovering as we develop these courses.

What are some strategies that can be used to encourage student engagement online?

We know that dropout rates have always been an issue for online courses. Keeping students engaged comes from the type of learning environment and learning activities you are going to offer them. They need to be related to the students' world, their values, their identities; but they also need to be challenging, to enhance curiosity, to create a desire to explore. Because our online language courses are for teenagers, we have videotaped a diversity of teenagers of different countries speaking the target language, to then create learning activities where the students explore and discover what teenagers in different countries think about issues relevant to them such as green issues, the virtual social world, music, etc. The learning the material is presented in such a way that the student is always kept active by making hypotheses, anticipating, creating, trying, etc. The tone of the course is respectful and who the student is, acknowledging that he has his own history, his own background, that he can bring into the course to accomplish activities where he is looking at his own culture, while learning about the target culture. We have tried to create a world where the student feels comfortable and motivated. This is also why we have developed a 3D world that models, in terms of architecture, the target culture, but in terms of activities, the dynamic that we can find in certain video games: students go on quests within the 3D world, they can take play different roles, such as be the waiter in a French café, they can interact with some characters in the 3D world. Knowing that teenagers enjoy these kind of playful although competitive 3D environments, we have created one in the target language and culture. This allows for the student to learn the language online and in a fun and safe environment, where taking risks is possible and encouraged.

How do you know that all is working well in your online classroom?

When things are working well — how do I know? The students are still there! (laughs) When they are filling more and more the self-assessment rubrics, when they spend more and more time online to work on activities and projects, when they participate more and longer during the weekly online synchronous meetings, when they start to ask to their online teachers questions such as "how can I do that?" instead of "why do I have such or such grade?". We also hope that students will spend more and more time in the 3D games to immerse themselves in this 3D world in the target language and culture. We have included a survey at the end of each unit in the course as a way for the student to tell us, regularly, how he feels in the course. But the best indicator, for me, is the kinds of questions students ask their online teacher. The type of feedback they are asking for is a good indication of where they are.

The role of the teacher in this environment is to be a guide— he's bringing feedback, he's the sounding board, he's the facilitator — he facilitates when he meets with the students and through feedback. The way he can follow the progress of his students and gives feedback, taking into account the development of the student over the long term, and the relationship that develops progressively, the tone of the comments he sends via emails, forums - respectful, warm, generous, inclusive – are all important elements to keep the students motivated and willing to go on with the online course.

CHAPTER 2

DOING IT RIGHT:
GOING BEYOND "BEST PRACTICE"

Non Satis Scire

(To Know Is Not Enough)

Now that we have discussed some fears and misconceptions that are shared by many teachers and trainers online, and have learned more about the distance learning environment, we are ready for action. It is extremely important to understand that teaching online is very different from teaching in a face-to-face classroom. We need to reconsider our understanding of the role of the teacher and trainer in this new context. An online teacher is not a giver of information as proposed by the modernist approach to education. Postmodern technologies require postmodern teaching, where the teacher is a negotiator of meaning, a resource, a facilitator in the process of the students' producing knowledge, rather than a "knowledge transferer" forcing the consumption of ideas and colonizing the learner's mind with her own world view.

Novo: What does modernism and postmodernism mean in learning?

Lauri: In modernist approaches to education, there were right and wrong answers and students absorbed correct knowledge like a sponge absorbing water from the fountain of knowledge, the teacher. The teacher, whose role was to be an authority, expected the learner to acquire and reiterate unquestionable facts. When the sponge was full, the lesson was learned. In postmodernist approaches, we understand that we think an answer is right because we have been convinced of this by sources of information that we perceive to be valid or well-founded. The right answer can change if we discover new and convincing knowledge from another source of information we consider to be legitimate. The teacher's role is to accompany the learner on a journey as the learner initiates and develops a piece of work. The teacher is a guide, resource, and negotiator, working with the learner to synthesize information and to express a valid and coherent perspective understood to be specific to that learning context and the learner's shifting sociocultural embeddedness.

"Old style" teachers believe that knowledge transfer is what they do. On the other hand, postmodern teachers will not only have to learn how to use different technologies, they will have to develop a whole new set of assumptions about what teaching is and how it works. Before you read this chapter, we want to point out that the problem for teachers is not just learning new technology: it is learning new technology and new pedagogy combined. This accounts for a large part of our fears: we sense, or we know, that not only our technical knowledge is obsolete, but our pedagogical knowledge is, too. When we are teaching at a distance, we realize that the way we have been teaching all our lives will greatly limit our students' learning and development online — and their engagement — just as it surely does in the classroom. Yet in the classroom we can get away with knowledge transfer because in a face-to-face context, where the institution and the teacher form a powerful presence, students mostly stay on regardless: there is no learner anonymity and it is more difficult politically and emotionally for a student to drop out.

Often we can't envisage transferring our teaching from the classroom to online, because our assumptions about how learning works are not adapted to the new technology. We need a shift from the right answer to the validly argued perspective, from the exercise to the project, from authority to guide and fellow learner — facilitating the learner's investigation of a topic and the generation of a well-argued and supported point of view with which we might not agree. We need a shift from being the controller to creating with our learners the interrelational conditions in which a learner's autonomy can develop and in which the learner can bloom: a golden climate, which will be discussed in detail in the following chapter. For now, we want you to understand that online teaching involves a different type of "doing" than traditional teaching, This is a crucial point, because without a postmodern mindset you will not be able to imagine how things will not fall apart online, or how teaching online can be successful.

A constructivist/postmodernist/post-structuralist approach is important to understanding how to be successful online, because it is important to understanding the value of project-based learning; the value of fostering learner autonomy; the value of not colonizing learners with one's own ideas about the way things are; the value of the person's initiating their own piece of work according to their own interests; the value of discussions about developing projects, ideas, arguments, etc. (social validation of ideas); the value of finding information and working out what is most important to one's project and arguing this; the value of reporting developments to peers; and the value of developing a perspective that is well-founded in the literature or experience, that is the person's own perspective, which might be at odds with everyone else's, including the teacher's.

Valuing this approach assumes that you show the learners that you trust them as responsible and independent individuals; that you respect and appreciate their expression of their own individuality in their work; that you will accompany them in developing interesting and challenging work; that you want to develop with them a relationship that is both intellectually and emotionally rewarding for everyone involved, including yourself; that you will give them feedback through constructive, perceptive, empathic, non-directive, and warm communication based on questioning and suggestion; and that you will encourage this form of constructive communicating and relating between learners. This is the essence of golden-climate pedagogy and the key to increasing connection, engagement, enjoyment, and performance online.

This chapter is designed to guide you through this shift in the perception of the way things are (ontology) and help you see the assumptions underpinning both how you are teaching now and the way you need to teach online in order to be successful. This part of the book will provide you with simple, practical strategies that are based on research in the fields of distance learning, psychology, business, and education. We are going to share some techniques that have been proven to increase the connection, engagement, and performance of the students online and promote your own enjoyment and happiness in this environment. We are also going to go beyond best practice, as we will share HOW to apply it so you get the best results. In this chapter, you will also hear the voices of the leading experts that will share their own practices and provide you with advice on particular issues.

Part 1: Three Secrets of Building Connection Online

Building connection online is probably one of the most important tasks for an online teacher/trainer. If you master this art you will be able to feel the invisible bond with your students, despite the physical distance that separates you. This link will build trust, help your students feel encouraged in their own search for meaning, and safely construct their knowledge through trial and error and in dialogue with their colleagues. It will provide a secure and validating basis upon which your trainees can build their own autonomy without feeling isolated, alone, or lost in cyberspace. Since your role as a teacher online is different from a traditional one, you will often find yourself reacting against the need to relinquish control and let your students struggle on imperfectly on their own. Your connection with your online participants is that pivotal dimension that will enable you to give up being the giver of knowledge and will help you foster a climate where your students are allowed to construct their own understanding of reality with your wise and gentle guidance.

Novo: Why should my trainees and students search for meaning? They are there to learn, not to navel-gaze!

Lauri: In life, you feel most engaged in an experience when you have a hand in constructing it. Like when you go to the cinema, you like to have a say in the film you see, right? Or when you buy shoes, would you like someone else just to give you a pair and say, "Put them on and keep quiet!"? No, you like to have a say. People feel alive, energized, and want to connect with the subject, trainer, and other participants when they feel curious to know about something. What they are curious to know about is what interests them, what contains themes and topics that are related to what they are living, or what they have lived — what is meaningful for them. Initiating and producing a piece of work is exciting; but it is also more complex and requires higher thought processes, such as critical evaluation and synthesis, than learning things that someone gives you to learn. At first the project can look like a tangle of ideas that might never come

together, so learners engaged in projects need to feel secure as they develop what they have found into a coherent piece of work. The teacher needs to focus completely on the learner's experience: to reassure, encourage, guide, suggest resources, and help develop ideas through discussing their meaning, implications, and perhaps ways of expressing them

Since online people have to build connections with someone whom they have never seen or most probably will never see in their lives, interactions in distance learning are very different from those that happen in a face-to-face environment. Indeed, there are specific psychological factors that are peculiar to this unique context. First, people's identity online might not be the same as in their offline life. Anyone can assume to "be" whomever they want to be and project only those features that they are pleased with, while hiding other, less attractive qualities behind the screen. The students and trainees have a choice of either letting others imagine their physical looks through the use of avatars that represent them, using their real pictures, or posting photos of someone else! This unique ability to set limits to your exposure is one of the most powerful features of the online environment. Because of visual anonymity, many online participants report feeling emotional safety that allows even shier students to contribute to group discussions and immerse themselves in conversation with their peers, something that they would have never done face-to-face. The flip side of this anonymity is that many online students and trainees feel more entitled to express opinions that might not be socially acceptable, and converse in an inappropriate or unprofessional manner. Trainers and teachers must use the power of anonymity to their advantage and carefully monitor and manage their students in order to build connections among online participants and avoid unpleasant situations that can lead to isolation online.

In this section we will talk about three secrets of creating online connection. We have put together an instant connection toolkit that will help you develop connection with your students from day one. We will then discuss the necessity of gaining learner attention from the start. We will provide attention-grabbing strategies that will allow you to win learners' interest right away. Second, we will talk about the power of your personal presence that will help you keep your learners' attention throughout the semester or the entire training session. Finally, we will share some tools that will help you diminish the "digital gap" and lessen the feeling of distance in your online classroom.

INSTANT CONNECTION TOOLKIT

SECRET 1: GET LEARNER'S ATTENTION

SECRET 2: ESTABLISH YOUR PRESENCE

SECRET 3: TRANSCEND CYBERSPACE

<u>Instant Connection Toolkit</u>

(If it's urgent, don't worry. Go to the EMERGENCY HOTLINE on page 51.)

A: About the Toolkit

You will never have a second chance to make a first impression

Most psychologists agree that it takes us about three seconds to evaluate someone when we meet them for the first time. Their appearance, body language, demeanor, clothes, smell, and gestures all create an instant composite image in our mind. It is as if our brain takes a quick picture of the newcomer that is immediately developed and is resistant to fading. Little nuances, such as well-polished shoes, a friendly smile, sensual aroma, or soggy handshake create an impression that quickly tells us whether this person is on "our team" or on the "opposite one." Whether he will hurt us or bring us joy, whether with him we will be motivated to learn and do well. Human perception is largely influenced by physical aspects, such as smell, sight, color, and touch and etc. However, how does one create the first impression online? How can we project our friendly, welcoming attitude, demonstrate our expertise and professionalism, earn trust and respect, and ensure our students' continued engagement and well-being when we are deprived of face-to-face interaction?

One of the reasons for high dropout rates online is the inability of the students to engage with the professor and others early on. This toolkit will help you set a positive tone in your online training session right away. It will allow you to connect with your audience and demonstrate your personality and professional qualities. Moreover, it will allow you to establish the foundations of The Golden Climate in Distance Learning, the secret to continued successful online teaching, which we will discuss in later chapters.

Before we proceed, we invite you to participate in the following exercise. It will help you develop your desired first impression online without being influenced by our suggestions. After reading this chapter, you can go back to this list and think of the ways that will best help you achieve these goals.

1. **What do you want your trainees to think of you online?**

_____

_____

_____

_____

_____

2. What are some qualities that you want to "transfer" to your students?

List:

_____

_____

_____

If you have some more time, here are some added questions to help you pre-pare for a successful start to your distance learning class:

3. Who do you want to be online?

1.   Get in the shoes of the learner. If you were a learner in this course…

a.   What would you like the teacher to be like?

_____

_____

b. Why is this important?

_____

_____

c. What would you want to learn?

_____

_____

d. Why is this important?

_____

_____

e. How would you want to learn?

_____

_____

f. Why is this important?

_____

_____

2. What is your ideal teaching self?

_____

_____

3. What would you like learners to say about you as a teacher?

_____

_____

4. How are you going to be that person, right from the beginning?

_____

_____

5. What is your ideal learner?

_____

_____

6. How are you going to help your learners be that person?

_____

_____

B: Emergency Hotline (relax, everything will be fine)

"I'm about to start a distance learning course and I need to..."

    a. seem competent

    b. communicate well

    c. handle discussions appropriately

    d. handle "difficult" students

    e. get a positive student evaluation

"I'm about to start a distance learning course and I need students to..."

    a. participate in discussions

    b. engage with course content

    c. communicate with one another and not become isolated

    d. communicate in a constructive manner

    e. communicate with me to clarify their understanding of materials

    f. communicate with me to discuss feedback

    g. communicate to me any difficulties they have in using the LMS

    h. stay in the course and not drop out

Then you need...

The Jumpstart Toolkit: The Eight Secrets of Instant Connection

1. Set up a warm and friendly atmosphere and show that you're just human, too.

    a.   Write something about your desk and your window and invite students to do the same [please see the example at the end of this section].

    b.   Add to 1a that you forgot something, have an ordinary view out of your window, have a small desk, have made a mess, have cold coffee on your desk, have noise on the street outside, etc.

    c.   Add to 1a that you long for chocolate or a Mars bar or salted peanuts, etc.

    d.   Write a short note back to the first people to reply, showing your warmth, humility, sense of humor, and understanding, for example, "Yum, dark chocolate," or, "Yes, it's great when the coffee machine's working," or, "Wow — you have the forest right out the back!"

2. Show that you're generous and thinking about the learners' well-being in the learning process.

    a.   Give a few tips early on about how to engage with the materials to prepare for discussions or for the first assessment. (Please see the example at the end of this section)

    b.   Invite people to contact you early if they think they might need extra time to do their assessments. Give them several ways to connect with you.

c. Invite people to contact you privately about any concerns they might have, no matter how small.

d. Reply as quickly as possible to learners' e-mails to you.

3. *Show that you're open to new ideas and not arrogant and set in your thinking.*

   a. Frame your responses as suggestions and put a question mark after what you write online, for example: "Perhaps, to the contrary, Hume (2008) meant that when in the presence of others, managers should show pride in their subordinates, rather than be critical?" The question mark will allow students to disagree with you more easily and will allow you to show that you are also learning from their opinions by building in their disagreements to your arguments.

   b. Draw learners' attention to a feedback form that will allow learners to tell you about their experience in your course, concerning both the material covered and your teaching approach.

   c. Learners can fill out a feedback form any time and send it to you.

4. *Encourage connectivity, collaboration, and mutual respect: show that you're confident that the other online learners are friendly, too.*

   a. Write that, "We're a warm and friendly bunch, so please go ahead and put up a question or ask if someone would like to swap ideas on anything, including work to hand in. " (In competitive classes, you need to have posted a note somewhere that learning from one another is fine, copying / plagiarism is not. Ideally, a few lines warning against plagiarism can be part of the cover page for each assessment to hand in, and students can sign it each time. You can also provide examples of what plagiarism is and what it is not).

5. *Show that your presentation will be clear and logical.*

Make sure

   a. the work to cover is clearly presented with short explanations
   b. participants can contact you easily
   c. the reason for the course and materials is clearly stated
   d. the expected outcomes are clearly stated
   e. the mode of assessment and each assessment is clearly described

6. *Show that you are aware of the politics of teaching.*

   a. Tell students that what you have selected for them to learn is a choice that you have made, according to your perspective on what is useful for them to learn in this subject area.
   b. Encourage students to read beyond the material you have presented to them to engage with in the course, and to present their findings to their colleagues for discussion.
   c. Tell students that the types of assessment and the assessment guidelines are a choice that you have made, and that you are aware that these forms of assessment might not correspond to everyone's preferred learning style.
   d. Encourage students to criticize the articles or chapters that you have presented to them to engage with on the basis of the following (this can also be an assignment):
       i.   inconsistencies in the logic of the argument

ii.   ii. inconsistencies between the introduction and the conclusion

iii.   weak sources of information (not peer-reviewed)

iv.   inadequate sources of peer-reviewed information

v.   weak referencing procedures (assertions not supported by references from peer-reviewed sources of information)

vi.   important questions that are not covered in the material

vii.   perspectives challenging the author's argument have not been considered

7. *Create ice-breaking activities.*

Use the first one or two classes to build connections among your trainees. In this way, students learn about each other and their teacher and are more comfortable contacting each other. (See examples at the end of the Chapter).

8. *Personalize your first interaction.*

Address all of your students by their names. You can create a generic welcoming e-mail and cut and paste the names of each student into it. It will take a little more of your time, but at the end it will be worth it. Your students will appreciate your efforts to relate to them as individuals and will feel valued and respected.

Where possible, call or e-mail each of your students on the first day of class, welcoming them to class.

Reply to students' first e-mails personally on the first two days of the course.

NOTE: In order to establish a connection from the start — one that sets the foundations for an optimal learning relationship with your students — you should understand that the first few days of classes are extremely important. You must free your schedule and be there for your students, using a so-called front-loading technique that requires you to be exceptionally helpful and available for your students. You should answer e-mails several times a day during this period and provide help as soon as a problem appears.

Do not worry, you will not have to dedicate your entire life to your online class. You can ease off your attention and provide less and less support to your students from the beginning of the second week of classes. However, if you can invest more time in the beginning, you will never regret it as you will be enjoying an engaging class where students can cultivate their autonomy in a safe environment that you have built with them. Remember, it is not only what you do with your learners that is important; it is how to be with them in a way that optimizes their engagement, enjoyment, and performance: that makes possible The Golden Climate in Distance Learning.

Examples:

1. Introductory text including friendly opening message, tips for engaging with the assessments/something about me as a person: my desk, my window

Tutor's e-mail to students:

Hi Everyone,

I'm Dr. Bill La Ganza, your friendly tutor. Please call me Bill. Students are generally a friendly bunch here online, all keen to work in well together and to get to know one another's interests and hopes and dreams. I hope that you find this course both interesting and challenging.

I suggest that as soon as possible you start to look at your assignments. Have a look under Assessment on the Home Page.

- What do you think a critical review is?
- What do you think the essay question means — what does "the link between citizenship and education" bring to mind?
- What kinds of research will you need to do to address the essay question?

When you read your readings, I suggest that you make notes about the parts of your readings that seem relevant for the three assignments. The relevant readings for the course are in your textbook, "Minority Perspectives...", and some are online in the library e-reserve at

http://www.lib.mq.edu.au/reserve

In other words, read your readings carefully, with the assignments in mind.

If possible, start writing your reviews and your essay soon; getting a first draft out is a good confidence-booster.

Especially with your essay, e-mail someone and tell them about your argument — the way you see concepts in the question to be connected, and what you have concluded. You will state this argument in the introduction of the essay, and it is very important to have one.

This is important: when you have worked out a conclusion to your essay — the way you think things are according to the essay question —, state this as your argument in the introduction to your essay.

So, who am I?

When we work online, it's a bit impersonal sometimes. One way to let people know a bit about yourself is to write something about where you work. For example, let your colleagues imagine you at your desk, working away, and looking out your window from time to time. The following is my posting about my desk and my window.

I invite you to do the same...

My desk, my window.

Hi Everyone,

I'm writing to you from an apartment in the Bastille quarter of Paris. A few days ago — well, this morning — my desk was a big mess, covered with chocolate crumbs, books, papers, files of ongoing projects, drawings from my daughter — the full "creative disarray" — until my partner blackmailed me by hiding my Lindt 85% cocoa and now my desk is the cleanest desk this side of the Seine. She was right, of course — my desk is our only table. But there are a few things creeping back, like a copy of the satirical newspaper I buy each week, a map of the coast where we're going camping in the summer on our bikes, an inner tube with a puncture, wires from my stereo that I've connected to my computer, and the speakers, and a plate that until very recently had a sliced nectarine on it. Ah, what do scientists say about entropy? Outside, it's a fine spring morning and the bar across the road between a vinyl record shop and a second-hand clothing shop will be quiet for another few hours — unless it rains.

Best wishes, and good luck for the course.

Bill

A typical student's posting in reply:

Hello,

I thought I should add a word or two. Sorry I haven't replied sooner – but I'll soon be moving. Only 22 days away. That's 3 weeks. MY GOSH!!! I just realized!

My desk is a mess. It doubles up as a laundry table! I have a pile of jeans and tops, tissues, a light, a clock-radio, a phone and charger, speakers, a music box from when I was 9 (love it!) I have three CDs that never use coz the music's on the HDD. But they are there anyway! =D I've got two leather journals with leather thonging that never stays tied up (I love my stationery!). An external disc (40 GB). A ball of paper that should be in the bin.

Oh, and my view? Well, the least boring window has trees as far as the eye can see (not far! =P). Two gum trees which are moving in the wind. Clothes should be dry soon.

Happy studying everyone!

Cya, Anastasia

Ice-breaking activities

One Lie and Two Truths. This activity asks the students to list three interesting things about themselves. They need to come up with two true statements and one lie (I flew a helicopter; Shakira once told me I dance well; and I can break one brick with my hand). Other students must vote to determine which statement is a lie. The student with the most incorrect votes from her classmates wins.

Interviewing. Ask the students to pair up and interview each other. The students will then report on what they discovered about each other.

Learning Styles. This is a useful activity not only because it works as an icebreaker but also because it helps the students reflect on their learning style and analyze the ways it can help and inhibit online learning. It also allows the students to form groups of like-minded people right away. The students need to take the test and then report their results and find students with similar learning styles/personalities. In their respective groups then they need to brainstorm their strengths in the online environment and discuss how they would overcome their challenges. Free learning styles survey: http://www.engr.ncsu.edu/learningstyles/ilsweb.html

Free personality survey: http://keirsey.com/

Secret #1: Get Learners' Attention

In a traditional setting, our brain only allows about eight seconds of focused attention at a time. In the context of distance learning our attention span is even shorter: we are even more prone to searching for information and finding distractions. The overwhelming majority of learners constantly browses the Internet or participates in their social networking groups during both synchronous and asynchronous classes. How do you get the "click'n'go" generation to "click'n'stay" in your training session?

Part of the answer lies in neuro-psychology as applied to the online educational context. Our brain needs stimulation in the form of curiosity, referred to by neuroscientist Jaak Panksepp (1998) as a "seeking" system of the brain, which is responsible for our continuous search for information and ideas. A busy brain that is trying to look for interesting information stimulates increased levels of the neurotransmitter dopamine, responsible for our sense of purposefulness and focused attention. Our neurons are even more excited when they cannot find any pattern, as our brains prefer stimulation over boredom. Therefore, the way to win your learners' attention is to provide novelty, emotional engagement, and unpredictability in your online courses. What is more, don't keep this secret to yourself — share it with your learners and empower them. They can use many of the ideas below to draw your attention, and that of their fellow participants, to their postings online. The more students feel they are making an impact online, the more connected they will be. After all, you want your learners to be producers of well-defended ideas as a result of the synthesis of information and engagement with others, not consumers of existing information.

Here are seven tools that you can use to gain learners' attention in a novel, emotionally engaging, and unpredictable way:

Tool #1: Follow visual design principles.

a. Color

Color plays an important role in getting your learners' attention. In order to create uniformity it is best to have a limited palette of colors associated with your course. Try to pick two main colors to establish your course "identity" — an accent color and a second color. The background color should be neutral. It should also complement the main colors. In order to draw attention to some important points you can use your accent color.

The accent color should draw attention to specific items on the page that you want to highlight. Remember we talked about the fact that our brain needs stimulation? Your accent color will use this psychological principle and instantly highlight your most important information! Remember to use it sparingly and only for the information that requires the most attention of your learners.

b. Images

Photos and images immediately draw people's attention. If you use a well-chosen photo at the beginning of your post, your students will dive right into the first paragraph of your text. An online course without images looks dull; and even the most interesting content gets lost in the continuous text!

However, not all images are created equal. Unless your image is directly related to your topic, your readers will either ignore it or get confused by it. A social marketing guru, Derek Halpern (www.socialtriggers.com), explains how wrongfully chosen images could hurt even a million-dollar marketing campaign. When T-Mobile chose to display Catherine Zeta-Jones on their website promoting their new, easy-to-dial phone, instead of selling more phones they only confused their customers. Certainly, Catherine was gorgeous as ever; however, an older shopper, who wanted to buy a phone with easy-to-press large buttons, was disappointed as she could not see the size of the buttons on any of the pictures. The problem was that Catherine Zeta-Jones' image was used for decorative purposes only. It grabbed the attention, but this attention did not serve the main goal of the campaign. Therefore, you want to implement ONLY the photos and pictures that clear-

ly communicate your message in your online course. Think as a marketer —
you are trying to promote the benefits of engaging with your content to your
students! Chose the images that support your message or add to it!

c. Fonts

Using too many different fonts can be overwhelming, besides the
fact that it does not look professional. We suggest choosing a maximum of
two fonts and only those that are easiest to read. This means that we need to
forget about fancy lettering: it is better to go with a "boring" but legible font
than to have pretty but confusing letters. Remember, you want your students and trainees to be able to read your content easily, and not to spend
hours decoding it.

Tool #2: Use the findings of eye movement research!

Positioning images in the "right" place is also important for getting students'
attention. Eye movement research shows how powerful this tool can be in
directing students' focus to where you need it. We interviewed James
Breeze for this book, who described his eye movement research in relation
to an advertisement to demonstrate the importance of placing images in the
"right" places. He notes that when a baby product ad used a photo of a baby
looking straight at the audience, readers paid less attention to the text, as
opposed to the same ad when the baby was looking at the most important
information.

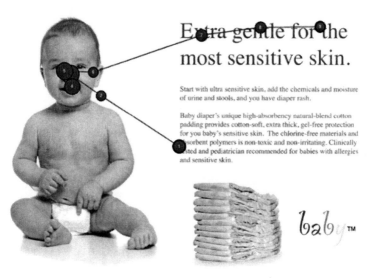

In the picture above, the sequence of the eye fixations is displayed by the consecutive numbers. As you can see, the reader starts looking in the middle of the page and then goes straight to the baby's face, where he focuses a few times, and then moves his attention over to the text. A different eye movement pattern can be noted in the same ad, but where the baby is looking up, toward the main content heading. Notice the difference: here the reader fixates much less on the baby's face and then moves to the text quickly.

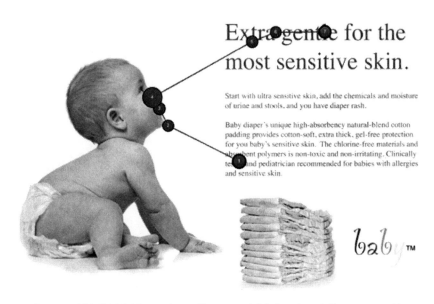

Extra gentle for the most sensitive skin.

Start with ultra sensitive skin, add the chemicals and moisture of urine and stools, and you have diaper rash.

Baby diaper's unique high-absorbency natural-blend cotton padding provides cotton-soft, extra thick, gel-free protection for you baby's sensitive skin. The chlorine-free materials and absorbent polymers is non-toxic and non-irritating. Clinically tested and pediatrician recommended for babies with allergies and sensitive skin.

baby ™

If you are not satisfied with the baby leakage protection, you will get your money back. Read more about our leakfree guarantee at www.baby.com

Now look at the picture below where Breeze combined heat maps of 106 people looking at the first image. The redder the spot, the more times people looked at it. As we can see, most of the focus is on the baby's face and not so much on the text.

In the next example, the same 106 people were looking at the second image for the same amount of time. (The images were shown to everyone in random order on Tobii Studio software running with a Tobii T60 Eye Tracker.) As you can easily see, many more people were reading the text in the second ad!

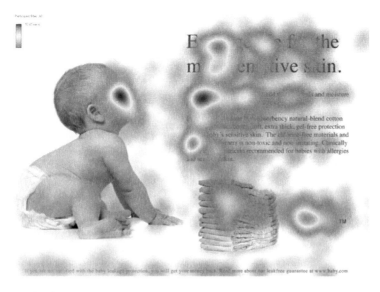

You can learn from this example and use images of faces in your course to get students to look at the most important information on your screen! We usually look at what the person we see is looking at. If they are looking out at us we will simply look back at them and not really anywhere else.

About James Breeze:

James Breeze is a CEO, Customer Experience and Eye Tracking Usability Consultant at Objective Digital. As an eye tracking specialist, James has used Tobii Eye Trackers for many years for market research and usability testing and has also helped universities with their academic research studies.

http://usableworld.com.au/2009/03/16/you-look-where-they-look/

Tool # 3: Use an engaging activity.

In order to get students' attention, include an attention-gaining activity at the beginning of the course. Icebreaker activities, a short video clip, a joke, a reflective question, a story, a case study — all of these activities are great lesson openers. You can invite reactions so that people can show something of themselves, share experiences, and identify colleagues with whom they would like to talk further — all of which serve to engender feelings of inclusion and connectedness, and overcome feelings of isolation. You yourself can engage in dialogue about the icebreaker activities, and perhaps in doing so share some personal information about yourself that can be interesting for your audience. Showing people you are human and that you trust them will definitely gain their attention.

Tool # 4: Make it all about the learner.

People love to talk about themselves, see themselves, hear their name, and pay attention to things that are important to them. Make it all about your learner: everything from guidelines and activities to graphics and references should be relevant to your students – perhaps reflecting particular cultural values and beliefs. People pay attention when their needs are met. Invite them to engage in an ongoing conversation about how the course or teaching might be adapted so as to better fit their needs, and make adjustments for your learners where possible. Suggest they might like to take an interactive test to generate their current personality type and learning style. Invite them to comment on the usefulness of these tests. This will start their habit of interacting with the educational platform. At the same time, it will provide you with information about your students that will allow you to connect with them during the course.

Creating conditions under which learners can take more control of the learning process will foster their autonomy. Autonomy in turn will encourage learner engagement, because when learning on an autonomous basis, they are active producers of knowledge and have a hand in a learning experience relevant to their interests. Where possible, make it clear to your learners that you will work with them so that they can influence as many aspects of the course as possible: the nature of their work to do, when they will hand it in, how much it is worth in the overall assessment, who they are working with, their sources of information, etc. Learners are most engaged in work that they have initiated, discuss regularly, and are directing individually or with others — work that involves exposure to a variety of perspectives and the synthesis of a response to the question at hand. You can encourage learners to share work among themselves for comment, even several times, before handing it in, so as to encourage the initiation and elaboration of ideas through constructive peer criticism (make sure at first they understand the rules concerning plagiarism). In this way, learners not only are constructing their own piece of work, but are making a contribution to the development and well-being of the whole group. The more the learner actively seeks information from reliable sources, or interacts with the course content, rather than just clicking to navigate to next screens, and the more the learner has agency and is involved in the social validation of ideas, the higher is his enjoyment and engagement.

Tool 5: Use a video for course navigation.

You will be surprised to know how many students dread working online because they are afraid to get lost in the learning management platform. If you record a mini video that shows students how to navigate through the course (you can use a screencast software to do it: http://mashable.com/2008/02/21/screencasting-video-tutorials/), you will get students' attention because

a. everyone loves videos,
b. you will take away their fear of being lost online.

Believe us, it is worth sacrificing some time at the beginning of the course to develop such a video. This video can be re-used for your other courses. It will also save you time during the course and will help you to avoid losing students who often drop out because of their fear of the online platform.

Tool 6: Craft a catchy headline.

Often, as teachers, we do not put too much time into developing titles for our posts and other materials that we want our students to read online. However, headlines and titles are almost like a face of your text. They are the first thing readers see and could become the only thing they see if they can't be bothered reading past your headlines. Your titles should go beyond pure topic description. They should not be long and boring, but rather succinct and to-the-point. The basic tenet for grabbing attention is to come up with a title that is interesting and unusual.

Follow the OCC principle when developing a catchy title. Your titles should be Original, Concise, and Clear!

Compare two titles:

Week 1: Introduction

Week 1: My desk, my window

Which title catches your interest?

Tool 7: Exploit that space!

Space is luxury. You are reminded of this when you are stuck in the uncomfortable seat on the airplane, wishing you could have afforded to buy extra leg room for your trans-Atlantic flight.

Space becomes especially important for your online presentations. Using written materials in the web-based courses is different from using them in the face-to-face classroom. In order to get students' attention, use that S P A C E!

Remember, you only have a few seconds to grab your students' attention; if your course is crowded, you will lose them. Approximately 64 percent of all readers skim over any online text, and if they are not instantly intrigued by it, it will divert their attention to some other distractions: posts, e-mails or social networking sites. Before judging your students for such hyper-minds, start paying attention to your own distractions. How often do you begin reading a text online and finish it without checking other screens on your computer? I bet you, not that often!

That is why you need to keep this fact in mind when writing for the web. To avoid all that hard work being wasted, you can use several strategies that will help you grab (and maintain) learners' attention. An online text should be easily "scan-able" but should not encourage your students to scan over some important points. Here are some steps to make your text web-ready:

a. Assign more space in the following ways on your course page:

Headroom: It is a good idea to add space above the course title and the main content area to visually separate them from the rest of the content.

Borders: Try using wider borders. Sometimes in our attempts to save space we create crowded pages that no one reads.

Text: When it comes to the text itself, we need to rewire our academic training regarding paragraph writing! Writing for the online course is different from writing for a textbook! Few course participants read from a screen the same way that they read from a book (we will talk about the psychology of online reading later on in the chapter). Try to open up as much space as possible. Read the paragraph aloud. Where do you use emphatic pauses? Add a space there!

b. Use a drop cap.

Many of us are used to seeing drop caps in printed texts. However, an interesting opening character that is larger than the rest of the text can attract the attention of the eye online and almost force your students to read. Therefore, larger characters coupled with an interesting introduction can hook a reader into the article. Also make sure that the text in your subheadings stands out from the crowd. Make your subheadings impossible to miss!

c. Don't make your side bar a focal center of students' attention.

While it's a good idea to include important information on the side bars, we must be careful not to distract the reader from the substance of the course, which is its content. Don't make your sidebar compete with your text. Your sidebar should have several important links that do not create clutter and confusion on the page. What is the most important spot on your site? Where do you want your reader to spend more time? Analyzing your site in this manner will help you set your priorities straight.

d. Use bullets.

In order to help your students see and retain important information contained in your text, try not to hide it by wrapping it in the words. If you place your bullets well, it will be almost impossible for the reader's eye to skim past them.

e. Use a good quote.

"I hate quotations. Tell me what you know." Ralph Waldo Emerson

Many people love the intelligence and simplicity of a good quote. Quotes are really great attention grabbers for your online texts. Finding a relevant, to-the-point quote is easy these days, just google your topic. Make sure that your quote really matches the core of your post, or provides a punch line for your story!

Secret # 2: Establish Your Online Presence

The concept of social presence was developed by J. Short, E. Williams, and B. Christie (1979) as a part of one of the first theories in communication media during the time when distance learning was in its rudimentary form. According to this theory, social presence can have various degrees of awareness of the other person in the communication medium along a one-dimensional continuum (with a face-to-face communication having the most social presence, and written communication the least). The most effective interactions occur when there is an appropriate level of social presence needed for the required task.

With the development of computer-mediated communication and more advanced systems of distance education, other views of social presence have evolved. Technological innovations have brought an entirely novel set of variables into the concept of social presence, and the post-structuralist understanding that social presence is constructed between the teacher and learner within their relationship has built upon this notion. One dimension of social presence is our availability to others, whether we show that we are able and willing to engage with our online community; another dimension concerns the way in which we represent ourselves online: the image that we project to others; and a third dimension is the feeling of community, or community climate, that is created online. All of these dimensions exist within the relationship that we establish with our learners.

According to the Community of Inquiry Model (Garrison, Anderson, and Archer, 2001), social and teaching presence are seen as the projection of teachers and learners who are involved in the negotiation of meaningful interactions. Since people differ in the way they perceive others, a sense of your presence will vary from one individual to another, and even within the same individual (depending on the day/time and her mood). Understanding your trainees' and students' personalities and learning styles can provide indications as to how you can communicate with them more effectively. Social presence needs to be considered in pedagogical design for distance learning because of the lack of physical cues. In a face-to-face environment, a teacher can still have a successful classroom without being aware of the need to develop her social presence, letting herself be guided by her intuition, whereas online, such lack of awareness almost guarantees failure.

A main goal of building your online presence is to reach the state where a media user no longer recognizes the role of technology in her experience (Lombard, 2000) and the distance disappears so the participants of the learning community can feel that they are "co-present" (Garrison, Anderson, and Archer, 2001). It is a challenging task, though, even for seasoned professionals, to reach transparency online and transcend cyberspace.

Web-based distance learning on an autonomous basis does not have to be an alienating experience for either the teacher or the learner. An important role of the teacher seeking to create an optimal online learning climate — The Golden Climate in Distance Learning — is to maintain the human quality of the teacher-learner relationship. This is achieved by letting the learner know that the teacher not only has that person in-mind, but recognizes the importance to that person of feeling "held" by the teaching context, including their constructing a firm identity as part of the classroom group. When the teacher communicates to the learner that she has the learner in-mind, the teaching-learning relationship is being maintained and the teacher confirms his presence. When the teacher is not present in this way, the learning experience is in danger of losing its educative quality and the learner is in danger of dropping out, not feeling "held" enough to learn and develop in the teaching-learning context that has been created. The definition of teacher's presence implies a paradox. A teacher in a face-to-face situation in a classroom might not be "present" for some learners. On the other hand, a teacher encouraging learner autonomy in distance learning, conscious of demonstrating to her learners that she has them in-mind, might be firmly present in their minds. These online learners can experience moments of constructive and reassuring inner dialogue with the teacher, creating a context conducive to a secure and enriching learning experience and learner autonomy.

In this section we will discuss the ways you can become aware of your online presence and consciously build it. First, we will describe how presence is related to the ability to be in the moment, or to be present. Second, we will discuss how your self-awareness will help you become authentic online, which, in turn, will build your strong online presence. Finally, we will talk about the power of the positive emotion for your online presence, and how in-mind teaching can help you be a reassuring and enriching presence in the learner's mind, even at a distance, and support the learner's presence in the learning experience. Building your presence online can be thought of as involving three interconnected phases:

BE PRESENT

BE YOURSELF

BE A PRESENT

Tool# 1: Be present.

Your online presence is felt strongly when you are fully present in the moment. The ability to fully "be there" is, unfortunately, a rare skill in our click'n'go society. Constantly distracted, our brains are in a continuous state of exhaustion and information overload. It becomes more difficult for us to concentrate on one thing for more than five minutes, and our attention is permanently divided between various activities. Often we are not even aware of the fact that we "coexist" in several cyber universes at the same time — checking e-mails on one screen, writing an article for a publication on the other, and checking students' work on yet another site. Imagine how you would be perceived in a face-to-face situation trying to have conversations with different people at the same time. Such hyper-mind functioning online is no longer considered rude or impolite. We even become proud of such abilities and braggingly refer to them as "multi-tasking."

Nevertheless, online or face-to-face, the image that you project onto others is only authentic if you are fully present in the moment. Perhaps you have experienced a truly "present" teacher, who captivated your attention from the moment she walked into the room, or showed up online. Even if you met this person many years ago, you can still vividly remember and imagine her and bring her presence from the past into the current moment. Perhaps you engage in an inner dialogue with this person from time to time when you need some extra strength to overcome a challenge. All of us can work on developing our capacity to be such powerful beings, who project a strong and inspiring presence to others, but to do so we need to be fully concerned about other people's perceptions of us and our effect on them in all aspects of our teaching approach, and reduce the time spent focusing on their effect on us and our particular needs. Consumed by constantly evolving technological gadgets, we often identify ourselves as being preoccupied with doing, and are not really aware of our being. Let us reveal several secrets that will help you become more aware and fully present in the moment.

a. Do one thing at a time.

Research suggests that we are more efficient when we dedicate ourselves completely to one thing at a time. Our presence is felt strongly even across cyberspace when we are fully involved in one activity. Therefore, dedicating time slots to your daily activities should be your priority. In order to avoid temptation, close all screens on your computer, not only when you teach a synchronous class, but also when you are teaching asynchronously (i.e., preparing a presentation for your students or correcting their work). Think about those situations when in a traditional classroom you were occupied by some worrisome or happy thoughts not related to your class. You probably recall how scattered your attention was, and how easily you could lose the grip of the class. The same situation occurs online. When you are actually being in the moment, by either teaching a class or developing online materials, you create a situation where the others feel, or will feel, that you are listening to them and they will take in what you are saying because you are literally present: you are paying attention. Besides, you will notice how your productivity rises with such an approach.

b. Use the 4 Cs principle.

A strong online presence is developed when, despite the distance, we can perceive the identity of the person that cannot be confused with anyone else. It is as if this person were in our immediate physical surroundings. Such powerful presence is established when we follow "the 4 Cs" principle: clarity, constancy, concern, consistency. Clarity is a function of how well you state your ideas, your objectives, and yourself. Can you identify your presence in a concise and concrete manner? Try to approach your online presence as a personal "brand." What do you want others to think of you? What features do you want to project? The beauty of the distance learning context is that we can show as much or as little of who we are as we want. We can actually hide our shortcomings and transfer only our strong characteristics. What are those characteristics for you? Ask your closest friends and your former students to identify you in three to five adjectives. Choose the ones that sound more like "you." Write them down on a note card. Read it often to remind yourself of who you are striving to be online.

Constancy is a continuous reminder of who you are and what you stand for. When your students know what to expect from you, they know that they can rely on you, and their connection with you becomes stronger. Have that card with your main characteristics attached to your computer and look at it every time you go online. Check often — are you clearly projecting those main features? In favorable learning conditions, constancy creates trust. Trust is a basic cohesive, relational element in distance learning and is experienced by learners when you are empowering, not colonizing them.

Concern is also necessary to creating a climate of trust with your students. If you show that you are concerned for their educative well-being, that you have them in mind and are thinking about how they are doing, anticipating their needs, showing empathy with their struggles and difficulties, then you are moving toward creating a Golden Climate in Distance Learning.

Consistency, another key element in developing a strong online presence, is the hardest one to maintain. "Do you walk your talk?" is a tough question for anyone. We follow our own advice most of the time, but do we do it 100 percent of the time? There is always room for improvement. However, trying to be consistent, constant, and clear 100 percent of the time — and always to show concern — will help you develop a powerful online presence and turn your aspirations into reality.

c. Use video.

In order to create the feeling of being there, it is important to use video. If you teach a synchronous class, try to show your face for at least some portion of the class. It sounds counterintuitive, but many teachers do not use video during their synchronous classes, despite the fact that video conferencing is an easy-to-implement tool. Video is important for any areas of study, but for some subjects it should be mandatory. For instance, in the field of foreign languages, video allows the learners to mimic teachers' pronunciation and assists with their listening comprehension. In any classes, video shows your emotion and your reactions to students' participation, which, of course, increases your presence. Even if you do not have the luxury of teaching in a synchronous manner, developing short videos for your online class will increase your sense of "being there," and will allow each student to learn about you and feel your presence — connect with you — at any moment.

d. Use social media.

Social media is another way to connect with your trainees and students. The growing number of social networking sites can be overwhelming for any teacher or trainer, but you can choose the ones that are easy for you to navigate and that fit your personality. Being present for your students outside of your classroom, even through a weekly reminder on Facebook or a short post on a twitter, will not only increase your online presence but will help you conquer new technologies and possibly even learn how to like these new technologies.

e. *Maintain virtual office hours*

The importance of assigning designated times when you can meet your students outside of their class to discuss their issues cannot be stressed enough. Online students must have a way to reach out to their teachers and have a way to connect in a synchronous manner. Even if the students do not actually visit you during your virtual office hours, the very possibility of contacting their professor allows them to feel safe and more connected to their trainer.

To understand better how to be present online for your students, we have conducted an interview with online presence specialist Dr. Rosemary Lehman. We hope you will enjoy this interview and will gain some valuable strategies on how to develop your own online presence.

Interview with Dr. Rosemary Lehman
Distance Learning Consultant and Author

Dr. Rosemary Lehman is a consultant in the field of distance education and a co-author of Creating a Sense of Presence in Online Teaching: How to "Be There" for Distance Learners (2010) and Managing Online Instructor Workload: Strategies for Finding Balance and Success (2011). For the past twenty years, she has worked for the University of Wisconsin-Extension, teaching and training faculty and staff, governmental and non-profit agencies, and business and industry in the use of technology for teaching and learning. She holds a PhD in distance education and adult learning and a master's in television and media critique from the University of Wisconsin-Madison. Learn more about Dr. Lehman and the books she co-authored with Dr. Simone Conceição: eInterface: www.einterface.me/eInterface.me/Home.html

Personal website: www.rosemarylehman.me/einterface/Home.html

What does online presence mean to you?

In our book we talk about three aspects of online presence: social, psychological, and emotional. Most people think of presence as a "thing," but it's really a process; and because it is a process it is more difficult to talk about it than about something more tangible. You need to create your presence before the course begins, during the course and after. And sometimes teachers continue to build their presence through follow-up.

You say that online presence can be developed before the course, during, and after. Could you give us an example, especially for before and after the course?

Before the course you develop your presence through designing your course. For example, you can include an orientation and also perhaps get in touch with your students before the course begins if you are lucky enough to have their names and their e-mail addresses and/or Facebook accounts. You can have some initial orientation activities that help students get to know other students. In this way you expand the length of the course by really thinking about it before the course begins, so when students come to the course they are "ready to go."

After the course you can do follow-up with your students. Sometimes this is possible, particularly in programs where students take more than one course within a program.

How do you know if someone has online presence?

There are certainly ways that you can measure this in your learning management system. Through self-reporting, students can let you know how they are doing, if they feel that you are connecting with them, and if you created presence for them. There are also other tools in the LMS. The discussion boards, the activities you use, the feedback learners give you when you ask for it can also determine if there has been a sense of presence created. However, I want to emphasize that presence is a process, so when you are in the course and students are responding to you and you are responding to then, you do get a sense of whether you are creating presence and if the students are present for you too. I think it is very important for people to be aware of their feelings, of how they think things are happening. For example, when I was doing a combined synchronous and asynchronous course, and we were in the synchronous aspect of the course, somebody at a remote site suddenly said: "Oh, my goodness, I thought we were in the same room! The technology seemed to disappear!" So it is a feeling, it is really not a tangible thing, but it is a "sense" that the student had because the course was well-planned, because everyone knew what they were doing, because activities engaged them and we were responding to them. So when they were fulfilling their needs in this course, all of a sudden they got this sense that they were really in a room face-to-face and we were not doing it via technology.

The same thing happens often in online courses. We have reports from our students that towards the end of the course they felt so engaged, and they felt so present, that we felt to them as "being there."

What are some strategies for creating strong online presence?

There are four types of strategies that we discuss in our book: design, support, teaching, and time allocation strategies. In the design strategies there are pre-planning techniques. With online and any distance learning courses you do much more pre-planning than you do in a face-to-face course. You need to have things written so that when the course starts you are ready to put your energy into the course. Anticipating your course responsibilities is also important, and having these laid out ahead of time and prioritizing course activities is crucial. Another part of the design is predicting your learners' needs; and the more you can find out about your learners' needs ahead of time the better you are. If you are teaching a course again, you need to spend time reflecting on the course you previously taught and revising it for the new context of the course you are going to be teaching and the new students that you will be having in that course. In support strategies, there is one-on-one support that you can provide for your learners and institutional support. There is also peer support where students are supporting each other; and then there is an external support, which would be the resources that you can provide your students with.

Among teaching strategies there are, of course, design strategies. Many of us still design our courses even though we might have some help from course designers. These also include administrative strategies since you need to think about how you will be administering your course, and the things you need to know for that. This is not so much about the content as it is about the logistics of the course. In addition, facilitating strategies are very important. You need to decide: Are you going to be a mentor during the course? a lecturer? a tutor? Are you going to facilitate what's happening? Are you going to mix these roles? So it is important to think about what your role is going to be. And of course, there is an evaluative part of it. How are you going to evaluate the course and what are the tools that you can use for evaluation?

We describe time allocation strategies in detail in our *book Managing Online Instructor Workload: Strategies for Finding Balance and Success* (2011). Briefly, they include being organized, being disciplined, distinguishing between your work and your personal life, which is very important because teaching online can be very overwhelming and you need to really set up your boundaries, and yet remain flexible.

What are some advantages of establishing online presence?

The main one I think is learner engagement and retention. It has been shown in the research that one of the main reasons for lack of retention online is that people feel isolated and that they feel that they are really disconnected. Based on this and other research, we have developed our definition of presence: the feeling of "being there" and "being with others" in the online environment. It is essential to keeping most students in the course, and of course meeting their needs as you are doing this. It is also about giving the students the sense that the course has been designed for them and their needs are being met, that you are very accessible, and that other learners are accessible as well.

What are some obstacles for developing online presence, and how to overcome them?

One of the major obstacles is the way we think. Those of us (and I am one of them) who learned to teach in a typical classroom think in a certain kind of way. We need to rethink our teaching, become more open-minded and more flexible, and look at the online environment as it is. We shouldn't try to recreate the traditional classroom online because the traditional classroom was created for a different environment. So I think being very flexible and having an open and creative mind is important. Another thing that is very necessary is visualization because you are not going to be right there with your students. You need to visualize your learners at remote locations and to try to put yourself in their shoes. One of the best pieces of advices that I received is that before you teach online, be an online learner, so that you know what your students are experiencing, and you can better adapt your teaching to that environment. Another obstacle is the lack of administrative support: inflexible policies, lack of funding, and lack of real understanding of what online teachers do. I don't think that the administrators who haven't taught online or who haven't taken an online course have a clue as to what's involved. That is why it is very important to have administrative support, that the instructors get sufficient funding, incentives, technical support, and training. Another obstacle (and I alluded to this before) is the tendency to have our online work take over our life. It's very important not to do that. You do have to create boundaries. You need to be very mindful of saving time for your family and for yourself. It's a real balancing act, but you do need to set the limits: letting your learners know when you are available and when you are not available, how soon you will respond and being very accessible but not overly accessible.

Do you think online presence is similar to your face-to-face presence?

There are some similarities, but the concept is entirely different. It's different in a variety of ways. It's different in space because you are not in the same space. It's different in time because you don't just have one scheduled class (in many cases, online students can access their class any time and you can do the same). The boundaries are also different: in the classroom you are within the walls; in an online classroom there are really no boundaries, everything is just "space." The way you use your senses is different because in the classroom everyone is there, you can see their body language, have eye contact. You cannot do that in the online environment.

So you need to adapt your senses and create ways to accommodate it. The level of interaction is also different. You need to plan ahead more online than in the classroom; and your level of planning is different. Your teaching effort is also different. You have to be very focused for different periods of time, whereas in the traditional classroom you need to be focused for about fifty minutes. Your focus and your teaching effort take much more energy online, particularly in synchronous teaching.

To conclude, I want to say that creating presence is very important: in the way that you create the learning experience for your learners and also in the way you respond to your learners.

Tool #2: Be yourself

In order to develop online presence it is important to develop a strong self-awareness and project the image that is true to who you are. You cannot create a solid presence if you follow one-size-fits-all "best practice." Your presence must be a living, breathing entity that matches your personality, your values, and evolves as you evolve, as opposed to being a stagnant façade. Your personal presence comes from within; your emotions help you project it across cyberspace. What is your personality? How does it help you (or hinder you) to be effective online? What aspects of your personality do you need to develop to be as effective as possible online? What is your preferred teaching style? How does it affect your choice of various educational technologies and activities within the LMS? How do you react when things get tough? How do you deal with a conflict? How do you motivate yourself every day? These are important questions to answer. In this section we provide you with suggestions and tools relevant to increasing your self-awareness.

a. Know your personality and your teaching style.

If you can harness something about yourself that can help learners to engage fully in the learning process and grow toward autonomy, your presence will shine through any distance. Seeking external perspectives on your personality is one way to start being aware of who you are, and reflecting on the kinds of learners you want your students to become, and how you are going to help them get there, is a way of understanding which aspects of your personality you need to develop in order to become the most effective teacher that you can be online. There are many ways to gain insight into your personality as an online teacher. You can try various free online personality tests, imagining yourself teaching online while you fill them out in order to give them a relevant context. One example, at http://www.123test.com/disc-personality-test/, allows you to identify and reflect on some weaknesses and strengths, so you can apply this knowledge to your teaching and training. Being aware of your weaknesses is important. As in the exercise above where you wrote down the features that you want to project online, we suggest that you might write down the qualities that you want to work on, and post them as a reminder on your computer screen. Take the tests again in six months' time and see how your personality is developing as an online teacher.

Your teaching/training style is an important component of your self-knowledge. Here are two free online test that will give you some indication as to the role you are currently playing online.

(http://www.gotoquiz.com/what_is_your_teaching_style_1)

(http://teachingperspectives.com/)

Once you have determined the style of teacher you are right now online, and have reflected on the kind of learning process you would like your students to experience, you will gain insight into how your teaching style might develop in order to become the most effective teacher that you can be online. You might also better understand your preferences for various educational technologies and features of the LMS — and consider some alternatives. Does your choice reflect your teaching style, or is it adjusted to the learning styles of your students? Do you position yourself in the center of the leaning community, or do you allow your students to guide their own learning experience? We will talk about the role of the teacher in distance learning in the following chapter, but for now being aware of your preferred teaching style will allow you to evaluate how it might develop in order to attain your aims for you and your students.

b.   Understand the way you fascinate.

Why are you captivated by some speakers but not by others? Why do you remember some people you met long ago, and forget others you just encountered? In a distracted, overcrowded world, how do some people whom you only come across for a short time manage to make a difference to your life? How do you create connection with your students? How do you present your material so when they leave your classroom they do not only remember it, but want to talk about it, think about it, get their hands on it, find related information, all the while engaged in an intense and emotionally charged experience that keeps them pursuing their investigations and projects? You are not going to achieve these results by purely providing information; you need to give your students something more.

A stellar marketing coach, Sally Hogshead (www.sallyhogshead.com), believes that fascination is the most powerful way to affect and inspire change in others. Sally believes that in all communication there are specific things that cause us to immediately focus and pay attention. She also suggests that we have control over this situation. Once you realize the way you fascinate, you will be able to create instant connection, get attention, establish your presence, and fascinate others. According to Hogshead there are seven triggers of fascination: power, passion, mystique, prestige, alarm, rebellion, and trust. You can have a preferred style of fascination, or can purposefully choose it depending on what kind of response you want to create with your audience. When your fascination trigger is power, you will take command of your environment. You will approach the task from the standpoint of authority. When you use the trigger of passion, you will attract with emotion. You will be able to encourage others through communicating your excitement and involving people's senses to paint the picture. When you use mystique, your task is to arouse curiosity, create situations where people want to fill in the blanks. Prestige triggers increase respect and elevate people's standards. The trigger of alarm creates urgency and the ability to drive people by using deadlines. Through rebellion you creatively present something traditional in a new light, providing a counterintuitive way and finding a different way to re-create it. Trust is built on consistency and reliability. When you use trust, people will know what to expect from the relationship.

Fascination plays a crucial role in every type of decision making. It is the power of creating messages that people not only listen to but act upon. Therefore, your role online (which we will discuss in more detail in the next chapter) is different from that in a traditional classroom. You are not an information provider, you are a relationship builder, whose goal is to connect with the students, engage them, show that you are concerned for their well-being in the learning process, that you trust in their ability to perform well and become strong and independent, and thus add value to the knowledge that they acquire from the course. Because of the addictive power of web-browsing, our students have developed a short attention span. Knowing how you fascinate will help you win their attention and build true connections. To test your predominant fascination style in your present online teaching context, here is a link to a free online test:

http://sallyhogshead.com/fscoreq1/

c. Learn about yourself from your failures.

All of us feel like failures occasionally. Most of us feel like failures quite often. Failure is something that in our society is considered shameful, and people try to avoid it as much as possible (and never admit to it). However, feeling like a failure is a natural stepping stone on your road to success. The way you react to difficult situations can tell you a lot about you! When things fall apart, do you also fall apart? Who are you when things get tough?

A renowned psychologist, Dr. Wayne Dyer, has a good way of illustrating this point. He often asks his audience a simple question: "If you squeeze an orange, what will you get?" Well, the answer is, of course, orange juice. No matter who squeezes the orange, how hard it is squeezed, and when it is squeezed, orange juice is what comes out of the orange because that is what is inside that orange! Similarly, the way to find out who you really are is to let yourself be "squeezed" by the circumstances. Do we tend to place responsibility on someone else, believing that our reactions to events lie outside of us? Dr. Dyer tries to demonstrate that our reactions are based on our internal state of emotion. If we express anger, then anger lies within us: if we react with kindness, then kindness is what we contain. Therefore, when life "squeezes" you, especially in the online environment, stop and think about what you are expressing in this particular context, or online teaching and learning climate, at this particular time. Is this the person you want to be and to project in cyberspace? How can you work on your reactions when you are not emotionally charged? How is your presence affected? How could you create a distance learning climate in which you could be the teacher that you would like to be? Understand that any successful person will feel like a failure at some point in life. Don't hide from the feeling, but acknowledge it, learn from your reactions, and find some tools that will help you deal with it in a way that will maintain your presence and will let it shine according to the image you have described for yourself above.

Novo: So, I can find out who I am and this will never change?

Lauri: "Who you really are" is continually renegotiated in a particular context (intersubjective, geographical, etc.) and over time. If we are going to develop our effectiveness as teachers in the online context, developing our personalities and teaching styles accordingly, then who we are will change, too. By the way, citrus fruits have evolved anti-fungal defenses that become active just after picking....

Tool #3: Be a "present."

What's the first thing people notice about you online? How does your presence feel to others in cyberspace? What do people remember about you? Some people are memorable for inciting unpleasant emotions, while others have something about them, or a je ne sais quoi, that is hard to describe in words. Do not be fooled by the medium of interaction in a web-based classroom. Your energy is strongly felt online and can be contagious. So how do you create a presence that feels more like a "present" than a "prison"? The convenient thing about online teaching and training is, thanks to your communicating via written and audiovisual communication that you carefully prepare, that you have time to present all the qualities that will lead to a successful online learning experience! As an online teacher you have a chance to present yourself in a variety of ways. Here are three secrets to how you can be a "present" to others online.

a. Be genuine.

One of the most honorable qualities in any person is the ability to be genuine. Online, this quality takes on an even greater importance. In a context where there is no physical connection, where members of the learning community often feel isolated and scared, it is important to know that the teacher or trainer behind the computer screen is someone you can trust. As you cannot provide a reassuring physical presence, building trust with your learners online takes more time than in a face-to-face environment. What is more, losing trust can be sudden indeed.

Being genuine — showing that you are a human with strengths and weaknesses — is important in building trust. At times this means showing your human failings, such as admitting mistakes or confessing that you don't have an answer right away. Being a genuine human also means that you are aware of your imperfections and are therefore compassionate toward and concerned for your students' well-being in their learning experience: you are not hypocritical. Students will forgive you for many things; however, they will not forgive you for not being genuine. It is important for them to know that they can rely on you, that no matter what the circumstances may be, you will remain the supportive and understanding person they have come to know as they struggle on through the cyber maze. When you create a welcoming climate that is based on trust — which comes from your ability to show authentic feelings and express the four Cs we discussed earlier — our students will be emotionally and intellectually present with you in a relationship that also legitimates and enables their connecting with others in an authentic way. They will engage in a way that sustains them in their educative experience; this will boost their self-esteem and their esteem for you as a teacher. In this way, you will earn the respect of your learners: they will listen to you, not because you are demanding, but because you have created a space in your relationship with them in which they, too, can be genuine. They will know that this is valued, and feel safe within a supportive climate that will allow them to expose their own vulnerabilities as they engage in the learning experience as novices.

b. *Choose your preferred medium.*

In a face-to-face learning context, our identity is partially expressed through the clothes that we wear, the hairstyle that we choose, or the way we put/throw/slide/place our bag on the ground before we sit down in the seminar room. In the online environment, you can also choose your own communication medium that can help you express who you are. In order to provide differentiation for your trainees and to account for various learning styles, you should consider using different types of media for presenting your content. What is more, you can choose your preferred media to communicate with your students on a regular basis.

There is a variety of media available that can highlight a specific attribute of your identity. Are you a blogger? You can express yourself via written discourse if you like to write. Do you like abstract representations? You can use visualization through symbolic reasoning, avatars, and graphics. Do you like moving images or public speaking? You can use video if you prefer a more spontaneous, natural form of communication. Do you like spontaneity and adventure? Then you can use synchronous discussion, such as chat. What about the wit of a few well-chosen words? You can tweet if you like communicating in mini bites, and, for those who like to mull, you can use message boards and e-mails if you enjoy deeper, more reflective forms of interaction. Ultimately, it is up to you to discover what your genuine identity is online, given the particularities of each teaching-learning context and what you wish to express to your students and trainees. In contrast to a face-to-face context, you might wish to emphasize some qualities over others and choose the medium that best matches your communication style.

c. Use your emotion.

The affective dimension of teaching and learning might seem less apparent in distance learning than in a face-to-face classroom. However, the affective dimension is highly important because it is the "glue" that ensures student/trainee engagement with their colleagues and the teacher, and that allows learning to occur and successful outcomes to be achieved. Distance learning is, in fact, an extremely emotional experience for both teachers and students. Even avatars with emotionally expressive faces can be beneficial to learners and trainees in a distance learning context. Avatars can promote learner motivation and engagement, and even make the learning environment more "personable." For example, Ortiz (2006) found that avatars that express emotions can raise student satisfaction and retention of knowledge.

As teachers, we need to be aware that, once online, we are emotionally transparent and our fellow participants can easily perceive our feelings and dispositions. The teacher's development and fine-tuning of the affective dimension of their teaching is the secret to creating the Golden Climate in Distance Learning that will be discussed in detail in a later chapter.

Our emotions do not exist separately from the emotions of our students. Any emotion is energy in motion. It is not only for your own sake that you need to stay positive and welcoming; you owe it to your students, too! It is important to set up a good "vibe" before you start your online class. Even when you teach or train in an asynchronous environment, you need to be aware of how your emotions affect your expectations and reactions and, hence, your presence. Our brains like to predict the course of events. In any conversation, they want to know what happens next. We often do not listen to what the other person is saying, but complete his thoughts with our own conclusions. We do not enter into further discussion with them and negotiate with them what meaning they are trying to communicate. Further, since we are also driven by a fight or flight response to any sense of danger, we withdraw or overreact when we are met with a perceived threat. Therefore, try to come to any contact with your online course (synchronous or asynchronous) only in a state of "calm receptivity." Do not correct papers, answer e-mails, or post anything when you are experiencing any strong negative or defensive emotions, or are unbalanced. Remember the transparency of this environment in which you are trying to be a present! Calm and open your mind first, and only then attend to your class. Interact with your students and with your LMS whenever you feel positive and receptive, and share your excitement, passions, and interests with the participants in your course. Remember, emotions are contagious, especially online. Share your positive energy with them: there is nothing more inspiring than being near someone who lives from their passion and joy. Be a present and you will connect with your students and foster positive feelings and openness, despite the distance.

One further dimension of being a present, as mentioned above, is communicating to your learners that you have them "in-mind": while not being physically present, you can be firmly present in their minds, allowing them to engage in constructive and reassuring inner dialogue with you, thus creating a context conducive to a secure and enriching learning experience. "In-mind" teaching, which involves communicating concern for the learner's educative experience and anticipation of the learner's educative needs, is important to constructing with your learners a Golden Climate in Distance Learning. This is described in more detail below.

Secret# 3: Transcending Cyberspace

Research shows that connection online is one of the key elements of a successful distance learning course (Berge, 1999; Higgins et al., 2001; Young, 2006), and the lack of such connection can lead to isolation, frustration, and higher dropout rates (Berge 1999; Hara & Kling 2000; Northrup, 2002). Most students admit to feeling isolated from their peers and teachers online, and express their negative attitude towards this feeling. Some of them even see isolation as an inevitable part of the online learning experience and believe that there is a "sacrifice" that one needs to make when taking an online class. Moreover, isolation can lead to fears of alienation, lack of communication, everything falling apart, and getting disorientated.

There are at least two forms of isolation: isolation from peers and the teacher, and isolation from the learning materials. Connecting with peers and the teacher, as well as with the learning management platform, is the key to transcending the feeling of isolation online. Providing students with the teacher's contact information is not enough; they might feel reluctant to communicate outside of the class, because they do not get to know one another as quickly as they might in a face-to-face classroom. In this section, we will disclose secrets that can help teachers and trainers to "transcend cyberspace" and diminish the distance in online classrooms.

Tool #1: Create an organized learning environment.

In a distance learning context, students often have to work on their own. It is frustrating if they cannot easily find homework assignments, locate a test, or review a course syllabus. Being lost online exacerbates the feeling of being lost in class. Indeed, many students confess that their learning experience is much more enjoyable when their teacher creates order and structure online. Easy access to all activities, deadlines, and the class schedule increases learners' sense of security, predictability, and trust, and reduces frustration, leaving students in a positive state of mind that promotes student connection. In a distance learning classroom, this makes their study a less isolated experience. When students log in to an organized, well-structured website, they feel welcome and encouraged by the teacher to learn, even in the asynchronous environment. In a synchronous classroom, it is also easier to follow the lesson that is organized and has consistent, recognizable parts. When students have to spend hours searching their class website for basic information, they feel that they are wasting time and are more likely to feel disconnected and unmotivated.

Tool #2: Provide extra resources.

Making extra resources available in distance learning provides more opportunities for learning and practice and enriches the experience of learning on an autonomous basis. According to a majority of students, one of the main differences between traditional and online learning is the lack of or limited opportunities for practice. To help students engage with their new materials on their own, provide a list of resources and links to some other websites. You will be surprised to see how many students actually explore these optional resources: just track their usage with your LMS.

Students also point out that when they are provided with different types of activities, exercises, and tutorials they feel more connected, more satisfied, and less isolated online. They like having the option of either reading a handout, watching a video, or downloading a podcast. The more variety the students have, the more chance they have to work on materials and activities adapted to their individual learning styles, and the better they learn. Students confirm that extra materials presented in different formats makes them feel as if they are enjoying the flexibility and richness of learning in a face-to-face classroom.

Tool # 3: Offer printed materials option.

Despite the fact that many bookstores are being closed and the nation is steadily shifting towards digital materials, a lot of students still prefer textbooks or hard copy handouts to reading from the screen. Many online schools have the course textbooks and all study materials uploaded directly to their LMS. However, printing numerous pages from a website is time consuming and costly for those who enjoy traditional reading. Provision of tangible materials solves this problem and allows anytime learning for students who do not like studying from their mobile devices. We need to remember that even "digital natives" sometimes do not like to log on to the computer and enter their virtual classroom every day. Students confess that because of the lack of printed texts, they do not put as much work into the course as they would like to. They explain that clearly organized printed materials make learning online more similar to learning in a traditional classroom.

Tool #4: Be accessible and available.

The accessibility and availability of the online teacher or trainer is vital for ensuring a student-teacher connection conducive to learning. Ideal online teachers, according to the students, are those who hold regular office hours, provide various forms of contact information, check their e-mail regularly, and respond to students' inquiries within twenty-four to forty-eight hours. It seems that the availability of the teacher is even more important than her quick correction of students' work. If teachers respond promptly to students' e-mails and let students know when their assignments will be graded, many students will feel reassured, comfortable, and content. The contrary is also true. Students describe a bad teacher as "someone whom you never hear from" and see such unavailability as a lack of care. Therefore, being able to easily contact a teacher who is available for help and answers on a regular basis seems to be crucial for transcending the distance and for increasing student satisfaction in the distance learning environment.

Tool #5: Develop rapport.

Creating connection and transcending cyberspace can also be facilitated through developing rapport with your students. Many students believe that personal communication, or rapport, with their teachers could make them feel more involved in their classes, more satisfied, and less isolated. Students value personal interaction with their professors and miss the ease with which such interactions occur in a traditional classroom. They can even perceive the lack of personal interaction as lack of care. As we mentioned earlier, in order to develop rapport, a teacher can use icebreaking activities at the beginning of the class so that students can learn about one another and their teacher. Course participants can also learn more about their teacher through a picture and a short biography posted on a website, through e-mails, and even through social networking sites, such as Facebook, Twitter, or MySpace. Research supports this idea and demonstrates that when teachers develop a rapport with students through personal communications, students have a better chance of having a successful online learning experience.

Tool #6: Deliver effective feedback.

Connection is a two-way path with which both teachers and students must be actively involved. Inability to give useful and prompt feedback increases the feeling of isolation and emphasizes the distance in the online classroom. Feedback can help you maintain the quality of connection that you build through your attention-grabbing initiatives and establishment of your online presence. However, not all feedback enhances the educative quality of your connections online. There are several features of effective feedback that you must adopt consistently in order to conquer the distance.

a.   Make it personal.

Offering personalized responses can create a sense of connection between the student and the teacher and lead to student satisfaction online. Students feel less isolated and less like "a number" when they are addressed by their name. Avoid as much as possible communicating with your students in a "Dear students…" manner. Spend a few extra minutes to insert your students' names into the general e-mails. When answering a student's posting on a bulletin board, you can begin your answer, "Hi Jane, Hi Everyone," so as to respect the writer and also the other participants by including them, too. In returning marked work, a pre-set template for grading your students' assignments is a useful idea for your personal time management, but you always need to reflect on a peculiar characteristic of your students' work. Detailed feedback showing the student what he did wrong and how to fix it is vital for students' learning and for their connection online. While marking electronic documents submitted by your trainees and students, using comment balloons to add reflections on specific aspects of your learners' work allows you both to paste in generic comments and write fresh responses to their ideas.

b. *Make it timely.*

Valuable feedback involves more than underlining mistakes and proposing possible solutions. It also needs to be given in a timely manner, while the student is still interested in learning from the teacher's response. Create a rule where you check your e-mails every day and send replies as soon as you receive a request. You do not need to come up with a detailed answer right away. Stating that you got students' questions and providing a time when you will send a full response will make students feel less isolated and lost online. The same thing is true for correcting students' homework. Don't be rushed into turning the papers around in twenty four hours. Create a reasonable limit that will allow you to avoid fatigue and a concomitant loss of quality. Most students will be comfortable with receiving their assignments at a later time as long as you communicate the exact time and stick to the deadline. In any case, if you have been able to show compassion and understanding for students' needs, particularly when they have had personal difficulties, they will do the same for you if ever you have trouble meeting a deadline.

c. *Be encouraging.*

Despite the fact that most students want to know what they are doing wrong, any criticism from the trainer or teacher needs to be framed in a constructive, positive tone. To maintain their engagement in a context in which there is not often immediate reward for their presence, ideas, or detailed contributions, learners need a lot of encouragement online. You need to communicate to your students and trainees that you understand that despite the difficulties inherent in learning online, they are doing a good job, that their contributions are valued, that their very presence online is valued, even if they are not yet contributing to discussions, otherwise they can lose interest and disconnect. Positive feedback has the capacity to provide students with a sense of belonging, to increase their motivation, and to improve their learning.

Novo: What's so hard about learning online?

Lauri: Learning online is a struggle for students and trainees for a lot of reasons. To be a successful online learner — to keep learning without immediate social contact or feedback — a person has to have the following capabilities. They need to be able to persist in developing a piece of work, negotiating appropriate directions with the teacher or collaborators; be methodical and disciplined; be logical and analytical; be reflective and self-aware; demonstrate curiosity, openness, and motivation; be flexible; be interdependent and interpersonally competent; be venturesome and creative; show confidence and have a positive self-concept; be interdependent and self-sufficient; have developed information-seeking and information-retrieval skills; have knowledge about, and skills in undertaking, the learning process; and develop and use criteria for evaluation.

Part 2: Three Secrets of Creating Engagement Online:

Learning can happen in a variety of ways, depending on the student, the subject to be learned, and the environment in which the learning takes place. As more courses come to the online landscape, it is increasingly clear that engagement is not just something to consider, but an essential part of the learning process. If a student isn't engaged, how will they play an active part in their own learning? What will stop them from dropping out of the course?

When, through formal learning, we develop a sensitivity to and understanding of new topics, we use a variety of different cognitive/affective processes. These include the following:

- creating
- problem solving
- reasoning
- integrating
- decision making
- evaluating

What you need to realize right now is that these processes are interrelated, involve both emotions and the intellect, and happen naturally when a person works toward finding a solution to a question. The journey from one process to the other would appear to be linear, though we understand that the human mind with its emotions continually shifts its focus as we anticipate and reflect. When exposed to a concept or problem that she needs to explore, a student creates a way in which she might learn, problem solves to see how she can approach the topic, uses her own reasoning processes to expand her knowledge through integrating perspectives from a variety of trusted sources, makes decisions on what she has learned, and evaluates her results. The outcomes of these processes, which vary according to the learner's personal, social, and physical context, can become impoverished when students are not interacting with one another on issues, perspectives, and concepts that are important to their work at hand. The student interacting with texts and projects alone might have trouble, not only with thinking through topics, but also with not being able to see all sides of a problem or the possible developments of an argument. Engaging students online is imperative for the teacher, in order to avoid isolation and develop active learning that includes an element of social validation. Reporting back to other students on the progress of their projects leads to constructive criticism and discussion, which validates the learner's arguments and perspectives, and enhances the conceptual richness of his work. In order to engage learners fully, the teacher must initiate a learning process in which there are so-cial/supportive, creative, and life/needs dimensions: in which they respec-tively relate, create, and donate.

a. Relate

Develop a context that is relevant to your trainees and students. Think of the titles that might attract their attention (we talked about this in the connection section). Provide a rationale for WHY they might be inter-ested in learning this particular information, and create the conditions — such as with My Desk, My Window — that make them curious to com-municate with one another from the first day. During the learning process, collaboration develops communication, planning, management, and social skills, which might be underdeveloped in students fresh from school, but are increasingly in demand in the workplace. During the collaboration process, students have to be able to clarify and verbalize their problems and state their needs. This, in turn, helps them to develop well-grounded solutions, as their claims and arguments are repeatedly validated through conversation. Collaboration also increases the motivation of students and their respect for diversity and for a variety of perspectives.

b. Create

Make learning creative and purposeful. Supporting and guiding students as they identify and set their own problem is effective, as the stu-dents will engage more when working on something that they have designed themselves and are producing themselves, than when solving a problem from a textbook. The initiation and production of a piece of work is a creative process in which the learner(s) has purpose and control. We will discuss the benefits of the problem-based approach later in this section.

c. Donate

Encourage students to make valuable contributions to their own lives during their learning process. Projects that are relevant to students' experience or ambitions, and which are presented to other students for discussion during and after development, bring meaning and purpose to distance learning. For this reason, authentic projects relevant to students' lives are motivating and satisfying, leading to increased self-esteem and engagement.

Engagement is enhanced if the learning process includes the following three elements:

- collaborative teams — relate
- project-based — create
- outside focus — donate

When engaging with a distance learning course, the learner goes on a journey including nine interrelated phases, which involve emotional and intellectual processes:

d. Nine phases of engagement

A. Novices: In this phase, learners either do not know how to use online media, interact through message boards or chat rooms, or do research using databases; or they seem anxious about using the online media at their disposal. They only appear to be comfortable searching for information online and using e-mail and word-processing programs.

B. Enthusiasts: In this phase, learners avidly adopt technology but are unaware of — or appear unaware of — the need to be cautious about what they reveal of themselves online. They might be comfortable posting pictures or talking about their lives online, without any apparent concern for safety issues.

C. Information seekers: In this phase, learners are reticent about sharing personal information or work online. When seeking information, they are more likely to reach out to a teacher than to their classmates; it seems to the teacher that they are asking more questions.

D. Overwhelmed: In this phase, learners are overwhelmed with the amount of interaction and information coming their way. They start avoiding chats and message boards because they get sucked into cyberspace and get distracted by various links.

E. Relationship builders: In this phase, learners are comfortable using social media and do so frequently, even cultivating an image as a leader and becoming an online hub. With various foci of interest online, the learner can easily be sidetracked and have troubles keeping up with her online tasks.

F. Collaborators: In this phase, learners seek collaboration with fellow classmates, and may want to involve students in group accounts and forums, helping to create more collaboration. Learners in this phase are more at ease balancing their online presence with coursework obligations.

G. Innovators: In this phase, learners seek to innovate: they are interested in focusing on new ways of interacting and influencing, and are comfortable with online media.

H. Interrelator: In this phase the learner maintains an interrelational climate (we will discuss this idea in the next chapter) with her teacher and is able to solve issues autonomously while at the same time not become isolated online. She understands that struggling is a part of the learning process and values her ability to solve issues on her own. At the same time, she catches herself when she starts feeling disconnected and communicates the need for more interaction to her teacher and her peers.

It is an advantage for students to be able to maintain an online engagement in the e, f, g, and h phases, which enable the learner to generate a climate of support with classmates and the teacher. So, what is the teacher's role in fostering this level of engagement? In the following section are several secrets that will help you build effective engagement in your online classroom.

Secret #1: Addressing Five Types of Online Engagement

Given the diversity of the student population online, it's clear that different types of engagement and interaction need to be available to facilitate learning. Moreover, individual students need to engage in a variety of ways — with other learners, with course content, with the teacher — in order to participate satisfactorily in the learning process. Engagement can be enhanced overall if learners are encouraged to persist in negotiating a learning experience that is adapted to their learning needs, and if they succeed, with the teacher, in creating a climate in which they feel secure and energized with a desire to learn.

In the traditional learning setting, there is a clear distinction between the learner and the teacher, with the teacher's role being the authoritative provider of knowledge to her students. In the absence of a face-to-face context in distance learning, the learner can experience traditional learning as being impoverished in its restricted perspectives and its disconnect from their needs and experiences. In order to optimize engagement in the online community and classroom, it's important to help students see they can learn from a variety of sources, including libraries, databases, carefully chosen materials from the web, and especially from one another, just as they might have in a study group with other students in a brick and mortar school. There are four tools for building four different types of engagement that can occur online, and each offers the opportunity for deeper learning and a more successful class outcome.

Tool 1: Building Learner-Learner Engagement

The learner-learner type of engagement is where students engage with each other. When you're teaching a class, introducing your students to each other as guides in their journey for knowledge is essential. Students from different backgrounds may not be well versed in their topic at hand, but they can offer new perspectives to expand the course's content. The most important part of developing learner-learner engagement is building trust between the learners. If there isn't a basic level of trust, there may not be authentic engagement. Students who are uncomfortable sharing or expressing with other students may not only limit their interactions, but they might also encounter feelings of isolation in their education, since they are less than keen to interact. Here are some ways in which trust can be built among the learners in your online classroom:

- Creating and utilizing social rapport. In the first weeks of a class, lead by example in encouraging your learners to interact with each other, beginning by sharing details about safe, familiar subjects. Hopefully, with the development through dialogue of trust, the frame of reference will expand to include their interests, weekends, work, etc. Informal social interactions may continue throughout the course and allow for more formal task-oriented discussions to have a personal level of engagement. Inviting students at the beginning of a course to talk about where they study and what they can see — to write about "My Desk, My Window" — as mentioned above, is a way of helping students to begin conversations among themselves that are more about building friendship than about coursework. The friendships formed in this way can underpin social cohesion when work needs to be discussed or tasks need to be shared.

- Encouraging group enthusiasm and optimism. Classes that use phrases like "our class", or encourage students to use "our virtual team" when referring to their workgroups help convey enthusiasm for their work together, and a sense of optimism. Using encouragement and positive messages, these teams are able to generate trust quickly and continue to maintain high levels of trust. Inviting teams to give themselves a name, state four values that they stand for, and describe the role of each team member — basic teambuilding — can engender friendly discussion, a sense of common identity and purpose, and trust before initiating a project.

High trust levels in the group have a lot of benefits and help the learners to do the following:

- Take initiative. When a member of the class speaks up, they take the initiative for the group. Others in the group are more likely to become a part of the conversation as a result. In groups without trust, the members are less likely to take initiative, while groups with high trust levels are able to share more frequently and start discussions when needed. In groups with high trust, the members are also more likely to take initiative in discussions, even without direction.

- Manage problems. Many groups who do not have high levels of trust may focus more on technical troubles or task clarity, rather than the task at hand. As trust is cultivated, members of the team are likely to help each other out, and to ensure everyone feels supported. Problem solving for technical issues can occur, allowing for everyone to feel as though their concerns are being addressed and they are being included, even when troubles are present.

- Learning. The teacher and each learner create a climate in their relationship that might or might not be conducive to learning. When trust is present in this climate, the learner can feel safe from destructive criticism and inconsistencies, able to take risks, able to take initiatives, and able to ask questions or make suggestions concerning any aspect of the learning process or subject matter. In the same way, learner-learner relationships that are characterized by trust facilitate a learner's learning from peers. Mutual trust and respect are vital to quality learner-learner and learner-teacher working relationships, and thus are vital to producing quality group and individual work.

There are several communication strategies that can maintain trust levels:

- Predicting communication. When team members are not communicating well with one another, this causes trust issues. If some team members do not feel that others are available for tasks, this can generate uneasy feelings between them. On the contrary, team members in high trust groups are always aware of the need to be trustworthy and respectful. Thus, it is important to encourage your students to flag to their group both absences and times for their future communications. For example, you might invite students to let others know when they will not be online or when they will respond to queries. This ensures that the group be available during times when tasks need to be completed, and allows teams to be aware when future lapses in communication may occur.

- Circulating e-mail addresses. Make sure that students have access to the e-mail addresses of their classmates or other ways of contacting each other so they can interact among themselves, as well.

- Offering timely and thoughtful responses. Ideally, members of the group should offer timely responses in a discussion to help others and to show their commitment to the group. The responses should be thoughtful, constructive, and responsive to the questions or comments posed, allowing everyone to make a positive contribution to the task-planning process or the discussion, without anyone feeling left out or that they are carrying a heavier load in the conversation. A teacher cannot expect a student to know what it is to be thoughtful and responsive. It is imperative that the teacher identify exactly what she wants the student's response to be.

Novo: Well, what do I tell learners about the kind of responses I would like them to post online?

Lauri: I'd say set down some guidelines at the beginning, so that responses are thoughtful, constructive, and timely, such as the following:

Bill of Etiquette in Distance Learning

When responding to a fellow classmate's posting, please do the following:

1. Respond as soon as possible after your classmate has posted her thoughts.
2. Refer to what your classmate said, <u>showing that you understand what your classmate is concerned about, even if you disagree intensely with her point of view, or there can be no scholarly discussion.</u>
3. [Optional] Refer to other relevant comments or materials.
4. State your point of view in a way that adds to or challenges what your classmate said in a polite, positive, scholarly, carefully argued, and constructive way, introducing materials to support your point of view.
5. Your comment must be beneficial to your classmates and the project or learning focus at hand.

- Assigning leadership roles. High trust teams are those that have leaders who are willing to be positive during discussions, even when other members of the group are not participating as expected or needed. These leadership roles will change from task to task, allowing everyone to step into the role and create ownership in the outcome of the group's task. Therefore, providing your students with a variety of possible roles during your course and allowing them to choose them and change them, through negotiation with their classmates, will increase learner engagement. From the beginning, make it known that you encourage students to help each other whenever a need arises, but that you are available should a solution need to be generated for larger problems.

- Focusing on tasks, not procedures. Some groups with low trust levels have situations in which the members will focus only on discussing what the procedures for completing tasks should be, rather than on the tasks themselves. In high trust groups, members are willing to speak up and bring the group back to the task at hand, helping to move away from simply social communication or nitpicking about procedures. Encourage students' communication with one another and create a system of rewards for it! It is important to be clear about communication expectations. Since it can be challenging to have everyone in the class interacting with one another and with the teacher, make sure there are some boundaries on how often you expect participation, e.g., one long post per week and five responses. Where possible, invite learner input on these boundaries at the beginning of the course, so that they see clearly that there is a culture of respect and trust, showing them that you have confidence in their judgment, that their experience is valued, and that they have a say in where they are going and how they are going to get there, thus encouraging their agency and autonomy — and their engagement. It can help to propose a clear schedule for communication, i.e., when people should post, when they should interact, how often they should interact, etc.
- Remaining calm during crises. The groups that have the highest levels of trust are those that can remain calm during group troubles. Even though every group will have an issue at some point, groups with high mutual trust are more able and willing to remain focused on what needs to be done. In high-trust groups where

members have fallen behind in their assignments, other members are likely to encourage these students to finish their work so that everyone can complete the unit and reflect on their learning process and conclusions. Guide your students to develop a contract for their group that encourages them to be supportive of each other. Encourage their agency in this process, including their identifying ways of making sure their group members stick to their contract.

Tool # 2: Building Learner-Teacher Engagement

Learner-teacher interaction is the direct communication that a teacher and student will have with each other during a particular course. This is the most recognizable interaction for the teacher. As mentioned above, it is easier for a learner to drop out of a course online than at an institution they attend regularly. There is not the risk of face-to-face embarrassment that might come from having to explain dropping out to teachers or fellow students, and the power of the institution is less apparent online than when a student is physically present in a seminar room or on campus. If you want your students to engage online, you need to do more than just colonize your trainees and learners with what you think is interesting subject matter, relevant exercises, and valid tests. Knowledge giving will not work; would you like your students to choose your next pair of shoes for you without consulting you? Would you feel that they respected your needs and trusted your judgment; would you feel the satisfaction of having gone through the process of discovery and evaluation, of living creatively and having a hand in your destiny?

The secret of engagement is this: you need to find a way of making your trainees and students feel that they are involved in a learning process that they own, that they have helped to construct, working on a piece of work that is relevant to their lives and interests, searching for information and finding in it what is of most interest and relevance for their piece of work, reporting the progress of their work to other students and benefiting from the feedback, giving constructive input that can help fellow students and trainees clarify the well-foundedness, concepts, and arguments in their work, being producers of knowledge rather than consumers of it: having a hand in their destiny and living creatively as they progress through the course. You need to move toward a teaching approach that takes account of the emotional needs of the learner: the need to have social interaction, the need to have a say in what they are working on, how they work on it, and what value it has, their need to feel trusted and respected, and their need to feel that they are growing through the learning process, not just learning more about the subject, but that they are becoming more independent and more capable as learners. Yes, you need to guide them, to show concern for their struggle in initiating and developing a piece of work, to support them on their journey as independent, productive, and connected learners, to discuss the parameters and learning goals of the course, to orientate them toward resources, to negotiate what things might mean, how a piece of work might develop, what deadlines might need to be met, which people might want to work on which projects; but you also need to know when to let your learners be—how at the same time to be present for them and to let them be. This is the Golden Paradox, and the key to creating with your learners The Golden Climate in Distance Learning, which we'll discuss below in detail.

There are a few steps you can take as you build your role in this Golden Climate as a guide, facilitator, negotiator, and resource:

- Create clear expectations. When you establish what your students can expect from you, they will be able to respond accordingly. Be clear about when you are going to be online, how you want to connect online, and the type of interaction they can expect from you during the course.

- Check in and respond quickly. It's essential that you check in with the message boards and chat rooms frequently to ensure that appropriately focused discussions are taking place. If a student contacts you, try to respond within twenty four hours.

- Be a real person. Introduce yourself and talk about why you are teaching the course. Show your personality and make sure the way your messages are written is the way that you would talk in real life.

- Establish a consistent and predictable rhythm of communication. Even though you are a facilitator more than a teacher, it is essential that you be available to students for questions or concerns in the role of a guide, negotiator, and resource. Students who do not hear back from teachers or who don't feel the teacher is involved might struggle with isolation and alienation, lose their motivation to learn, become silent, or drop out.

- Start strong. The first week of your class is the most important in terms of fostering engagement. During this time, make sure you are checking into the site frequently during the day, as this will help learners see you as being present and engaged in the course.

- Create routines. From the start of your class, you should create a routine for handling messages, responses, and questions. At the very least, you should read messages and respond to your groups twice a week. This might be on Mondays or Fridays or midweek. This routine not only allows you to be up to date on what's happening in the course, but it also prevents large numbers of messages from piling up.

- Friday messages. A positive way to create interaction between the teacher and the learner is to have regular messages. On Fridays, make sure to post something that will help you gauge the progress of the class, as well as the participation. You might talk about the connections that learners made between the current week's topics and the previous week's lessons. You can also use this time to check participation and archive the previous week's posts. This is also the time to remind students what they should be discussing online so they stay on course during the following week.

- Tuesday night/Wednesday morning messages. In this message, you will be discussing your observations of the current discussion. It's a good idea to recap what has been said, particularly legitimating the expression of minority or dissenting points of view, and then ask questions of the group as a whole, based on the direction of the discussion.

- Facilitate learners' expression and interaction. As you become a part of the conversation, it's a good idea to keep in mind that rather than take over the discussion, it will be more inclusive and vibrant if you act as the facilitator of the discussion. Students should interact with each other more than they interact with you directly. When a controversial message is posted, wait for other students to respond before giving your response. When you give your response, frame it as a question that will stimulate deeper thinking on the topic.

- Keep messages succinct. When writing messages on the forums, you can model the proper etiquette by being succinct and concise in what you say. Say what needs to be said, but nothing more, allowing students to take up more of the discussion than you do.

- Write carefully. Think about what the goal of your message is, how the message will be perceived, and how it might impact others.

- Offer constructive and stimulating feedback. If you notice that a student might benefit from feedback, offer constructive feedback that does not dismiss their ideas but offers a new perspective to consider and stimulates their curiosity. In this way, you will help the student to expand her thinking on issues and concepts, and to appreciate some of the implications of her ideas. End your comments with a question mark so as to invite further discussion and show that you are a fellow explorer, and not someone who thinks they know all the answer. Know-it-alls block conversations and discussions by preventing scholarly inquiry.

- Consider class progress. When reviewing students' messages consider the progress of their learning and what you might do in order to propel them in a new direction or a direction that is more in line with your class goals.

- Be courteous. Whenever you interact with students, address them by their names, avoid using ALL CAPS, as it feels you ARE YELLING at your students, and use basic manners. Remember, students can feel isolated, but when you treat them as human beings, you allow them to feel like they are a part of a class, not just a message board, and they are more likely to engage in discussions and coursework.

How to Compose a Good Facilitating Message

Analyze post trends. While reading the posts of your students, try to identify the main trends or themes and jot down a list of questions that might deepen this conversation

Identify ways to deepen conversations. Navigate discussion so it has one focus and a narrow goal. Strive for depth rather than breadth of information when focusing on students' problem solving. Formulate your post as a question that probes the assumptions underpinning perspectives.

Legitimate dissenting or minority perspectives. Pick up on dissenting or minority messages that might have been sidelined or rejected by the mainstream discussion and legitimate their expression by bringing them up again for consideration. What might be the merits of each of these points of view? Are they founded on valid information? What are the assumptions underpinning each perspective? Why might they be threatening to mainstream interests?

Model behavior. Try to follow what you preach. Everything about you, including your messages, needs to reflect the standards by which you evaluate your students.

Think outside of yourself. Once you have written a post, set it aside and reread it as if you were reading it for the first time. Is it clear? Is it emotionally charged? What feeling does it provoke? Does it express the desired perspective? Will it whet the students' appetite for further investigation?

Establish guidelines for giving constructive feedback, so that you provide your students with clear ways to correct their work without losing confidence. Here are some suggestions on how to give constructive feedback.

- Reread what you've written. Before you send a message to anyone in your group, make sure to re-read what you've written. If the message includes criticism, think about how you might feel if you were to receive the message. Would you find it helpful, respectful, or insightful? Would you feel like contacting the person and thanking them for their sensitivity, understanding, and insight, and telling them that it would help you prepare a better piece of work? If not, hold off from sending the message for a while, and then think about if you would really like to send it.
- Show empathy. Wherever possible, show the author of the comments that you are criticizing that you understand their point and appreciate why they have made it. This will allow for a scholarly discussion based on mutual respect and understanding, and will prepare both the author and yourself for a possible change in perspective without losing face.
- Write to others privately. If an issue comes up that involves just one other person, write your message privately to that person, instead of posting it on the larger message board and cc-ing it in the e-mail. In order to help your students in this regard, you might post the following message:

- Re: Clarifying criticism. If you feel that something a classmate has written is an unfair, negative, or unconstructive criticism of you or your work, bear in mind that it is easy to misunderstand a person's tone, intentions, and meaning, when all you have is a written text. Even if you feel injured, e-mail the person privately and politely ask them to clarify their meaning on a couple of points and, where possible, to give examples to support what they are talking about. For example, you could write, "Hi James. Thanks for your comments about my project. In order to help me benefit from your feedback in developing my work, and if you still think that what you wrote is justified, please clarify what you meant by 'It's too technical,' 'there is no clear argument,' and 'the information is inaccurate.' Please give me some explicit examples of how I could make improvements. Regards, Sally".

- Use "I feel" statements. When writing constructive feedback, focus on using "I" statements, e.g., "I feel that this is happening," "I am affected when this happens." These statements are less likely to create defensive responses, as the writer is allowing for the possibility that only they feel this way, and the tone is not accusatory.

- Start with something positive. Try to begin with identifying something positive in every piece of constructive criticism. Commenting on something that works will help to generate trust and goodwill. In general, it is a good strategy to "sandwich" your critical comments, i.e., start with a positive note, add your criticism, and finish on a positive note.

- Support what you say with evidence. Include quotations or examples from the work you are criticizing so as to give substance to your claims and clearly show how improvements might be made.

Criticism that is unsubstantiated and that makes no effort to identify the author's intention and how it might be improved is of little value.

- Think about your impact. If you've been writing messages that convey criticism, without offering any constructive ideas, without acknowledging that other people's ideas have helped further your thinking, or without asking for feedback from others concerning your ideas, then your messages will have created uncertainty and anxiety without contributing to solutions or engendering a culture of trust and generosity. Encouragement, generosity, and recognition are needed from the teacher to maintain learner engagement in distance learning.

- Ask about feedback-sharing preferences. Discuss and negotiate feedback guidelines with the group as a whole. To what extent should feedback be revealed to group members? Some people would rather get feedback privately and only share it if they think it would be useful to the group as a whole.

Remember that discussions will occur online if, with your students, you have managed to generate a climate of mutual trust and respect, in which students feel safe to ask any question or put forward any idea, in which fresh thinking is valued and explored and criticism is empathic and constructive. Having achieved this climate, there are further ways that you can facilitate discussions online between students:

- Summarize. After many messages have been posted, it can be difficult for students to see patterns or themes. Summarizing the discussion helps students stay on track. If there are conflicts in data, for example, pointing them out and asking why they exist allows students to explain their thinking. In the summaries, ending with a question mark is best since this allows for the possibility that other perspectives are legitimate and invites further contributions from learners.

- Prompt. When you notice that a topic or a question is being overlooked in a discussion, you might gently prompt the students to draw their attention to this point. If a discussion has become quiet, you might introduce a new open-ended question to generate interest in the topic again.

- Guide. When you notice that a point of discussion has been overlooked, it may be helpful to orientate students toward this point. For example, you might say, "I noticed that the issues of federalism and the establishment of a common treasury with the power to tax have been overlooked in the conversation about the Greek financial crisis and the future of the EEC. What are your thoughts on this?"

- Moderate. Sometimes, focus can be challenging in discussions with multiple threads. Suggesting that students might like to focus on a certain point allows them to have a deeper, more nuanced, and more targeted discussion.

Tool # 3: Building Learner-Content Engagement

Learner-content engagement refers to the learner's accessing and drawing from the content texts of the course ideas relevant to discussions or his piece of work. Using your LMS as simply a content management tool creates a one-directional, and passive, use of this system. The course content (syllabus, outlines, discussion points, etc.), stored in your LMS, can also be used as tools for social or interactive learning. By facilitating engagement between the content and students, and interaction between students concerning the content, the students engage in an interactive learning process enriched by discussion and the various perspectives of their classmates. Through facilitating discussions and project work enriched by students' engagement with course content and with each other's perspectives, you guide students toward the course goals. Other sources of information might also be valid, such as peer-reviewed literature from journals and books and multimedia web material from reliable sources such as large learning institutions.

Remember, this is not a teaching approach in which you tell students where to go to find answers; rather, you encourage them to explore the parameters of an issue, raise questions, and go to the course content and other valid sources of information to find their own answers. Also, understand that distance learning is not only student-centered, it is student-driven. Allow the students to create their own content! This will ensure their engagement with the course.

Novo: What is peer-reviewed literature?

Lauri: When a person wants to make a contribution to a field of thought, they might write an article, a chapter, or a whole book. If they want people to respect what they write as a valid contribution to the field, they send their work to a publisher who puts it through a review process in which other experts in the field read and comment on the piece of work. The author usually has to clarify, re-write, and find additional sources of information before her peers are satisfied that the piece of work is well-founded, well-argued, and brings something new to thinking in the field. This rigorous process of review by established experts is called the peer-review process.

In most online classes, the class website has already been created for students to use. Devising ways to encourage them to visit it is the key to its success as a learning tool. Encourage students to visit the website regularly to post messages, interact with others, post assignments, etc. By assigning points for their interaction online and creating scenarios where students cannot avoid accessing their website, you will increase student-content interaction. The regular visits to the website in turn will allow for more interaction with the content, as well as with other students. On the other hand, not assigning points for online participation legitimates a difference in learning styles and does not penalize students who are shy. In this case, the assessments need to ensure that students interact with course materials in order to pass. Critical reviews of important papers, or essay questions that demand a nuanced understanding of the themes covered in course materials, along with weekly discussions of key papers that offer the advantage to participants of clarifying points and arguments that they can use in their assessments, can complement this approach and ensure a rich learning process.

At the beginning, student introductions, if they are substantial and relevant to the course, can be set as assessments and contribute to the grade for course participation. For example, one of the most effective first day assignments in an English language course is an "avatar introduction," as it allows students to share their personal information in English without feeling too "exposed" online:

AVATAR INTRODUCTION

Choose your avatar to "represent" you for the day!

Do you want your avatar to speak Russian? Arabic? Italian? French? Do you want it to have short red hair, a pair of fun glasses, and a Chanel necklace?

Do you want to be on the streets of London or practicing in Shaolin Temple in China? Tell us why you chose this particular avatar. Make a post that justifies your choice so we can learn more about YOU! I can't wait to see you in your new avatar.

To select your avatar for a day go to the website:
http://www.voki.com/create.php

When writing assignments, make the guidelines clear for students. You should always provide evaluation criteria for any assignment. The assignments should be challenging and you should offer feedback as well as grades on the assignments when turned in. Assignment questions that require the student to explore the literature, and on the basis of their reading to argue a point of view in answer to the question, require higher-order thinking skills such as problem formulation, decision making, synthesis of ideas from a variety of resources, constructing a position, and summarizing. You might offer a variety of questions for group assignments so that groups can choose a question, which engages the team early on in a process of debate, revealing some of the dynamics of the group. Individuals and groups can negotiate with your changes in the question, the number of words, the deadline for handing work in, and, if appropriate, what percentage of the overall assessment the assignment is worth, should you wish to encourage autonomy within your virtual classroom.

It is also helpful to use current events as starting points for online discussions and to encourage students to take charge of some discussions as well. An online learning climate characterized by trust, mutual respect, enjoyment, and the valuing of new, unusual, and dissenting ideas, in which the teacher is present but not seeking to influence the learners, creates conditions conducive to the learner's taking the risk to take control of their learning. Further, students will take control of their learning most effectively when assigned one of several clearly defined roles, each one providing a way to participate effectively in a discussion.

If students want to pursue interaction with online content outside the classroom, these sites can be a helpful starting point:

- www.merlot.org
- www.learner.org
- www.pbs.org/teachersource/
- http://ocw.mit.edu/index.html

Tool #4: Building Learner-LMS Engagement

The LMS you will use is important in the learning process: it is a part of the learning community, as the learner must engage with it. As the teacher, your responsibility is to facilitate interaction between the LMS and the student. Since the LMS can seem like a system that is one-sided — more of interest to the teacher than to the learner — your goal should be to create more interaction opportunities for the student so that they are continuously going back to the LMS during the course. In this way, they will come to appreciate the value of the LMS to the learning process.

As we stated before, the dropout rates of online students are 20 percent to 50 percent higher than those who are on campus. Creating with your students The Golden Climate in Distance Learning (discussed in detail in the following chapter) can greatly reduce the dropout rate, and part of this is helping students to experience the LMS as being an asset that supports their independence and the flexibility of the learning process, rather than as being scary and confusing. To become aware of individual students' issues in this regard, and to show that this is a priority for you as a concerned teacher wanting continuous improvement, create a "How can we do better?" discussion. In this discussion, invite students' comments on the culture of online learning, its strengths and its limitations, and ask for suggestions on how their current learning experience might be improved. Students' feeling that you are concerned for their well-being in the learning process is an important element in maintaining their engagement online. Don't worry if they vent their frustrations: as with face-to-face teaching, you won't be able to deliver a totally satisfactory learning experience for all students, and all students know this. The important thing here is that you show sincerely that you are listening to them, that you care, that you understand their issues, and that you are trying to find a solution. It's better to have a frustrated student continuing than an alienated student who has dropped out. Over time, student-LMS interaction will become seamless, as the student simply logs in and starts to learn, without prompting. In order to reach this phase quickly and minimize early dropouts, here are some more strategies that will encourage student engagement with the LMS and overcome their fear of technology:

- Navigation tools. When the course begins, provide your students with a .pdf or video navigation guide that describes the current LMS technology and its functions.

- Initial prompts. When the course begins, tell your students that they need to log in daily: they need to maintain continual contact with the system so that they can get up-to-date information about the class.

- Follow ups. Try to follow up with students after the first day and the first week to see how much they are logging in, if they are having any difficulties, etc. Check your "I want to do better" message board every day so as to reinforce your belief in a "continuous improvement" culture.

- Clear guidelines. The clearer your guidelines, the easier it will be for your students to use the LMS.

- FAQs. It can be helpful to create a list of frequently asked questions in a document file for students to have on hand, should they encounter trouble in the LMS.

- Access to help if needed. If the student has troubles with the LMS, make sure they have a way to contact you, other students, or tech support to sort out the problem.

By taking on the role of the facilitator and modeling your own use of the LMS, students will be able to learn within this environment, without feeling out of step with others in the class. When you recognize the five different types of engagement and you make a conscious effort to facilitate their use in the classroom setting, you provide multiple avenues for enriching the learning process and experience.

Tool #5: Building Learner-Learning Process Engagement

Students need to feel that the learning process respects their needs and that they are trusted to have a say in what they learn and how: they need to feel that they have agency and that you are fostering their autonomy. Let students know that all aspects of the learning process are available for negotiation, including the focus and content of their assignments, the percentage accorded to each piece of work that gets a mark, deadlines for work to be handed in, the composition of groups for group activities, etiquette guidelines concerning online postings, among others. When students know that they are an important part of their own learning process, which they have helped to design according to their specific needs, they will be engaged in it and will be less likely to disconnect and withdraw from your course.

Secret #2: Building an Online Community

Together, the different kinds of engagement described above can build a solid online community. To ensure that your learning community stays engaged, you need to realize that facilitating connections is about more than setting up a website, posting some assignments, and creating clear goals. Within the online learning community, there are opportunities to facilitate learners' substantial engagement with one another, even if they never meet in real life.

Tool #1: Setting Up Effective Group Dynamics

Before you can begin effective teaching in an online community, you need to understand that the key to success in distance learning is mainly existential: it is not about what to do with students; it is about how to be with them. Establishing a rapport with students based on trust, respect, engagement, autonomy, and enjoyment in the learning process establishes a way of interrelating, or a group dynamic that is conducive to learning. Students and teachers need to have this quality of rapport with one another so that they can take the risk of asking questions, making suggestions, putting forward dissenting views, making ostensibly tenuous arguments, and asking for help when it is needed. There are several strategies that can ensure that you initiate a positive group dynamic:

- Be humble — You can model the idea that you are not just a know-it-all teacher by being humble in interactions with others. Contribute your ideas, but be willing to listen to others' ideas as well. Putting a question mark at the end of your suggestions and comments shows that you understand that there might be other valid perspectives or questions to be asked. The "How can we do better?" discussion board mentioned above communicates your sincerity in regard to wanting to improve your approach, too.

- Be interested in personal details. Focus on building personal relationships when possible. Ask about how their weeks are going, what the weather's like where they are, how their families are doing, etc.

- Be open to other points of view. Always be open to alternate points of view, showing that you can understand how the claim made could be the case, even if you don't agree with it, and go on to state the reasons for your opposition. Disagreement with some claims in set textbooks or course readings legitimates critical thinking and the questioning of "experts." The "truth" can be talked about as a valid perspective, founded on trustworthy sources of information, of which we have become convinced.

- Set boundaries for discussions and interactions. Have students discuss the setting of boundaries for what will and what will not be a part of discussions. Within the bounds might be aspects such as using professional language, avoiding personal attacks, preventing sharing of information outside the class, etc.

- Take responsibility. When you make a contribution to a discussion that is ill-phrased or taken badly, take responsibility for the words said and own up to your own shortcomings. The best way to deal with anger directed at you is to act with compassion, understanding, and sensitivity to the fears and anxieties out of which the anger has probably arisen.

- Express gratitude. Be thankful to others when they have said something that you appreciate.

- Live up to expectations. If you say you will do something, do it. If there are rules, follow them. You have to walk your talk in order for students to know what to expect from you, which builds trust in you.

- Trust and respect your students. Show your trainees and students that they can participate in shaping the learning process and try to give them as many opportunities as possible to do this. In this way, support your students as they develop in their relationship with you and their capacity to learn on an autonomous basis, and as they become more independent and self-reliant.

At the end of each course, it can also help to share what you thought each student brought to the class and how that was valuable to you as the facilitator. Making a teacher evaluation questionnaire available to students so that they can comment on the teaching approach and their learning experience is also a gesture that can show your concern for students' well-being in the learning process, help students to feel expressed, and bring to light important issues of which the teacher might not have been aware. Students will know that their contribution will benefit both the teaching staff and future learners,

Tool # 2: Supporting Online Collaboration

Once you have established a relationship with your students that is conducive to a positive online learning environment, it's your job to create opportunities for them to collaborate with one another. Student-student collaboration strengthens relationships between students. Students will learn from one another and enhance their interpersonal communication skills and independent learning skills. Depending on the kind of work the students do and how they develop it, they can further enhance skills, understandings, and personal qualities associated with planning, negotiating, debating, implementing, demonstrating, and reflecting.

Apart from students' working together on pieces of work to be assessed, the following activities can help to foster online collaboration: class blog, class website, class podcast, database management, mind maps, self-assessment activities, games and puzzles, study groups, article reviews, research papers, case studies, discussion forums, interviews, surveys, etc.

Tool #3: Building Teams

While a part of collaboration, building teams will allow your students to have healthy competition and instant group connections to help them in their learning. There are a few factors to consider when creating the team dynamic:

- Team communication. As the teacher, you should provide clear guidelines about what is to happen on the team, how the team members are to communicate, and what the goal of the process is. These guidelines can be open for negotiation, so that teams can personalize their way of working while doing a particular assignment.

- Team selection. It's easier, faster, and clearer for everyone involved if teachers assign students to teams, rather than engaging in a lengthy student-student team-forming process. Having students fill out surveys beforehand about their favorite role when doing a team project, and their least favorite role, will help a teacher create balanced teams. On the other hand, allowing students a certain time to form their own teams, and then entering into the process to make sure the teams are well set up, allows for more communication and negotiation between students, early team engagement in the project at hand and in team roles and processes, and more autonomy.

- Team size. Student teams of four are most effective on small pieces of work up to two thousand words, or with a few clearly defined sections, and five to six students are most effective on longer or more complex projects.

- Team roles. Within the team, it will be necessary to define roles so that certain tasks are accomplished on time. Having the team develop a project plan, with team members, roles, division of tasks, and timeline showing the sequence of work that needs to be done, can help the team to bond and see clearly how they will achieve their task.

- Team bonding. Having fun exercises for students to do before the "real" work begins can help them bond and learn more about how they can work together. Further, as mentioned above, inviting teams to give themselves a name and state four values that they stand for — and perhaps to put these values in a "team shield" — can engender friendly discussion, a sense of common identity and purpose, and trust before initiating a project.

- Team rules. The teams may want to create a system of rules that will help define individual responsibilities.

- Team notes. It can help for teams to keep records of what they have done and how they have accomplished those goals. Turning in these notes will help teams stay on task with their projects. If your course has individual assessment, individuals need to keep a diary of how the team worked together to realize their project and particularly of their own contribution to the team. Reading the diaries of all the team members will help you to decide the worth of individual contributions to the collective piece of work.

- Team purpose. The function of teams can vary depending on the aims of the course.

   - Where grasping the salient points and core issues of a subject is important, a team project approach might be chosen to expose the student to a greater variety of perspectives from both the course materials and fellow team members than if the students were to work individually. Team members define the work to be done, divide up tasks, and make a synthesis of their efforts to form the final project to be sent in to the teacher.

   - Where the individual's relating the subject matter to their own lives is a priority, teams might be formed to act as support groups for team members as they initiate and develop individual projects. Team members would regularly report back to the team on the progress of their individual projects — "What's been done and where it's going" — and present the final result to the team for comment before sending it to the teacher.

Tool #4: Educating about online etiquette (Netiquette)

As students begin to interact online, it becomes clear that a set of rules peculiar to the online context needs to be followed. Online etiquette, or netiquette, is a set of guidelines that helps students be respectful to each other in communication. Here is an example of etiquette rules that you can provide your students with at the beginning of a course:

- Do unto others. This classic rule also applies with online communication, if not more so, as the lack of visual cues can easily lead to perceptions of criticism or aggression. Invite everyone to treat one another as they wish to be treated.

- Ask for clarification. If you think that someone is being aggressive or criticizing you, give them the benefit of the doubt and ask in a friendly way for clarification of what they meant.

- Be succinct. When talking online, just as in any other conversation, encourage students to listen more and talk less. Taking up too much space in an online message board can come across as being chatty, superficial, self-important, and domineering.

- Listen more. Being a know-it-all can disrupt the flow of online discussions. Even if you know a lot about the topic under discussion, listen for a perspective that challenges your own or adds something to your own, and ask a short question in order to expand your understanding of the topic even further. Why are you doing the course, if it isn't to learn?

- Be clear. Focus on saying what you mean, instead of being ambiguous. Reread messages before you post them to make sure you are saying things clearly and precisely.

- Avoid CCing. When speaking via e-mail, avoid including anyone in the conversation that isn't involved. No one wants more e-mail in their in-box than is necessary.

- Prevent plagiarism. If sharing something that is not in your own words, make sure to reference the material correctly.

- Speak up. If you have something that you could contribute to a conversation, or if you could answer a question someone else asks, do so.

- Be clear about humor and sarcasm. Though you might want to make a joke, realize this might not work out as well via message boards and e-mails. Instead, make sure you indicate that something is a joke or that you're using sarcasm to ensure the right tone. Or just avoid humor and sarcasm altogether.

When you build an online community, you build a landscape in which students can not only grow but can learn from each other and live their lives more fully. Facilitating positive and productive online communities is a process of building trust, putting people together, encouraging autonomy, negotiating meaningful projects, and watching learning take flight.

Secret #3: Project-Enhanced Learning

One of the most effective approaches used in the online environment is project-enhanced learning. When students are offered the opportunity to learn about a topic or explore a question, but in their own unique manner, they can use learning and problem-solving skills they already have and develop new abilities that will help them achieve real-life goals.

Project-enhanced learning is based upon post-structuralist assumptions that have to do with why learners engage in a course and how they learn. In traditional learning approaches, learners attempt to find an answer to a question set by the teacher, that the teacher supposedly knows about: learners try to guess the teacher's perspective. On the other hand, project learning involves learners in developing a piece of work, perhaps in association with other learners, in order to investigate a topic of interest to themselves. Importantly, many aspects of this project, such as the topic, length, value, due date, or collaborators, might have been negotiated with the teacher.

The learner(s) are not finding an answer to something that the teacher already "knows"; rather, it is assumed that the learner or learners might well find information that the teacher doesn't know about, in which the teacher will be interested for her own learning experience as a participant in the learning process. The project will, drawing upon a variety of media, present, discuss, and conclude upon various perspectives on a topic, each of them validated by being supported by peer-reviewed literature or literature from reliable sources of information. The perspectives might not be those shared by the teacher; what is important is that they be supported by references from the academic literature or government sources in order to qualify as valid.

The teacher has several important roles: a guide, helping to orientate the learner(s) and their project according to learner(s)' interests; a resource, pointing out sources of information that might constructively inform the project; a negotiator, discussing with the learner(s) all aspects of the project so that it meets their needs; and a facilitator, overseeing the development of the project and foreseeing obstacles where possible in order to help the project reach a completion that is satisfactory to all learners working on it. In order to create a learning climate conducive to fostering learner autonomy, the teacher can put all parameters up for negotiation, including the topic, the marks the piece of work is worth, the deadline, the project team members, and the length of the project. It is assumed that, being an investigation, a project will take its own course in unexpected ways. For this reason, the teacher will need to engage in frequent discussions during project construction concerning the direction of the project, team members' roles, mapping the project with task sequences, and deadlines: a continual re-negotiation of what needs to be done, why, for when, and by whom. Project-enhanced learning also means that through student interaction and learning on an autonomous basis, a learner observes firsthand and can integrate to his advantage a variety of learning styles. In a nutshell, a project is an inquiry into a topic that is multi-perspectival, multimedia, multi-student, and encourages the learners' autonomy.

In order to launch a project-enhanced learning process, teachers can create a list of topics or questions whose investigation would meet the aims of the course, and negotiate with students the manner in which they might produce a response. You might also want to provide summaries of past projects so students can see how other classes have approached their projects, and to get ideas on how they might want to begin planning and structuring their assignment. Rather than set up projects at the start of class, begin them once the class has had a chance to become familiar with each other's strengths. It can help to start off with smaller topics to explore as a team, and then have those teams come back to the class with results. With project-enhanced learning, the students become active learners who are looking for answers outside of the classroom, with the help of their classmates.

For any project, it is important to establish an authentic focus by placing students in situations where learning comes alive: where it is related to real-life experience. An example is sociology or marketing students focusing, for their project, on analyzing current advertising messages in the city's subway system in order to compare them with projected trends in the literature. A non-authentic experience would be to analyze advertising messages chosen by the teacher from a textbook, rather than analyze those in the real-life context. The authentic focus is the more engaging, as it relates directly to learners' current lived experience.

To orientate students toward authentic activities that are relevant, challenging, enjoyable, and engaging, teachers might emphasize the following when suggesting assignments for deeper focus:

- Real-world application. When students can apply their learning to real-world situations, interacting with society at large, they are relating their learning to current interests and experiences, and have more reason to engage deeply in their learning.

- Vague assignments. When you suggest an area of inquiry, concepts, or issues that might be explored — rather than set a clearly defined question — you can enter into a dialogue/negotiation with students in order to formulate in detail the topic or question they are to explore in their project.

- Long-term complex tasks. Assignments that are conceptually complex, that require broad and detailed investigation, or that involve the use of several kinds of media provide excellent opportunities for students to go into a topic or issue in depth and develop their capacity to work on an autonomous basis. Ensure careful initial planning so that projects don't run overtime; such projects can take longer to complete.

- Multi-perspective activities. Activities that require students to draw conclusions on the basis of a variety of perspectives will allow for deeper understanding of and sensitivity to an issue.

- Collaborative assignments. Assignments where students must work in groups to initiate, plan, produce, and present a coherent and well-referenced piece of work allow for a broad and deep collective focus, as well as develop a variety of high-level thinking and interpersonal skills.

- Cross-subject activities. Tasks that involve more than one subject of interest to the learner or can be applied in more than one situation of relevance to the learner are more engaging.
- Inner reflection. If students have to think about, or take notes on, their own learning experience while working on a project individually or with others, as well as their impact on the experience of other students or groups, this can help to enrich the learning process and enhance student engagement.
- Creative activities. While working toward accomplishing a goal initially identified by the teacher, but perhaps re-negotiated by the learners according to their particular needs, learners are given the chance to create different routes to that goal. Learners need support in this endeavor: they need to trust the teacher, the learning process, and other learners they might be working with, in order to conceive of, execute, and conclude a piece of work in response to the goal.
- Multi-perspective assignments. Some assignments might request multiple perspectives or solutions in response to the same issue, so long as they are supported with evidence from valid sources and fall within the original project guidelines.

Engaging online is about more than simply logging into a website and completing assignments on time. By creating opportunities for students to reach outside of themselves — to connect with other students and society at large in real-life situations — you create a deeper understanding of the world even as you foster independent learning practices that can serve the student after they complete the course.

Part 3: Five Secrets of Increasing Learner Performance

While online learning has become more popular in the past few years, the academic community does not always accept its educative value. Online learning is often examined for flaws and criticized, because student outcomes do not meet expectations and teachers feel that they have failed.

The truth is that online learning does pose a new set of challenges for teachers and educators. Some of them include

- physical separation from students;
- dependence on technological know-how and familiarity;
- larger class sizes;
- larger dropout rate;
- lower overall quality of student response and performance;
- feelings of isolation and alienation experienced by both students and teachers.

The above factors can reduce the quality of teacher-student and student-student interactions, and of student-student collaborative learning, which can in turn reduce performance. Distance education requires teachers to think about how best to adapt their pedagogy to the online medium as well as to students' academic and existential needs in order to optimize student performance throughout the learning process. When this is done, results ensue: distance learning can outperform traditional teaching methods. Importantly, educators require a new set of tools in order to generate a distance learning climate conducive to effective outcomes for their students. In this section we will describe four tools that will help you increase student performance.

Secret #1: Providing Differentiation

Online educators need to realize that different students may require different teaching methods in order to perform as well as they can. Not every student learns in the same way, and approaching students with only one teaching method will not be effective. Online education offers an opportunity for teachers to adapt the learning process to the needs of each student through teacher-student dialogue. The content can be expressed through a variety of forms, such as written text, video, audio, simulations, and tutorials. Thanks to technology, it becomes easier for teachers to assess which learning methods correspond to particular student's learning styles, and to respond to any changes in learning styles throughout the course. Educators can set up a variety of lesson modules offering links, games, polls, forums, tests, surveys, and more, allowing students to progress through the material at their own pace. The more the student is able to adapt all aspects of the learning process to their own learning needs and preferences, through negotiating these with the teacher, using the teacher as a guide, facilitator, and resource, the more the student is empowered in their learning experience and is learning under conditions conducive to successful outcomes.

From a practical standpoint, you might set out a course for corporate or university students that is structured, but then offer up some of those structures for negotiation (e.g., the assessment questions, the nature of work to be done to complete them, their percentage value, their length, their due dates, group or individual work, etc.). This way, you can adapt important aspects of the learning process to individual needs. It is useful to ask students who negotiate changes with you to include the changes to be made in an e-mail to which you can give your written agreement. This is a useful way to begin to loosen up structures in your distance learning courses, until you become comfortable with negotiating multiple aspects of the learning experience with your students.

Another way is to begin the course without structure, and then negotiate the structures that individual participants need to optimize their learning experience. In the case of an online corporate training course on change management, for example, the trainer might make available, when the course begins, a variety of materials in a variety of media, in order to allow the participants to interact with these materials. The trainer might make one initial request: "In order to move forward in this course, I have made a change: I am no longer setting you the assessments to be completed. You will do this yourself. In order to assist you in moving forward on this task, I have put at your disposal some articles, videos, and audio lectures on the subject of change management. Please e-mail me before the end of next week to let me know how you would like to proceed. What kinds of tasks, for example, would you like to complete, with what specific areas of focus in each task, worth what percentage each, and with whom?"

When each participant contacts the trainer, he or she can discuss possibilities concerning the assignment or assignments to be completed: and the trainer can ask the learner to spend some more time looking at the materials so as to fine-tune a direction for their work. Some participants might be anxious or even angry at the lack of structure and demand that the trainer clearly define the learning process: "What do you want us to do with the materials? What are the tasks and how is assessment organized? Do we work individually or in groups? Just tell me exactly what you want; I haven't got all day." Others might feel that there is too much structure and not enough information in a certain area. They might demand that they be allowed to look further afield for information before they can decide what information can best help them respond to their current change management situation: "You think this is the be all and end all of change management? What about information specific to our industry and to a large company? What about economic information? Four of us want to do a project on managing an acquisition."

After receiving feedback from all participants, the trainer might hold a short debriefing on learning styles: How did each participant want to manage their learning? Did they want more or less teacher involvement, more or less independence? Also, what about the learning experience as an experience of "change"? How did each participant cope with the existential aspects of change? How did they feel when given limited information and limited orientation concerning the coming change?

On the basis of the reflection on learning styles and existential experience, the trainer might declare that "all aspects of the work to be done and its value are still up for discussion on an individual level. In order to move toward formulating topics for assessment tasks, let's discuss what you have found in the materials that is important to know about change management, and why you think it is important. I'll make a few suggestions, too. Let's generate a list of topics and then open a discussion board for each topic so we can see who's interested in exploring what area in more depth and come up with assessment questions for individuals or groups." In this way, the trainer can continue to work with participants on adapting their learning experience to their needs throughout the seminars, building on their self-knowledge as learners and fostering their independence.

Secret #2: Creating Effective Presentations

Presentation is the key to success in communicating with others, and clear, substantial work that is logical, plausible, and thought-provoking is compelling and essential to high performance in assessments. Presentation is also important in whetting your students' appetites for discussion and setting an example of how you would like them to communicate in their assessments. Think of your subject area as something that you are passionate about, like a beautiful house, of which you have visited a few rooms and would like to visit more along with your students. The first impression is important, so you would like to introduce them to the house in a way that excites their imagination and curiosity, so that they want to stay, marvel, explore further, and learn everything about it. It is the wanting to learn that will keep a student persisting, despite setbacks and dead-ends, in finding, synthesizing, and presenting information, and which makes high grades possible.

If you aim to optimize student performance, the way you present your content is crucial. While it might be tempting to believe there is a certain standard way in which you ought to present information, the best way to present is rather personal, intersubjective, and contextual. Below are some tips to help improve the way you offer lessons to students. Think about the last PowerPoint presentation you observed. We often learn that to create a good PowerPoint presentation we need to come up with five to six bullet points per slide. While the clearly-marked points may have helped guide the presenter, they may not have engaged the listeners, who can easily "zone out" and forget material if it is presented in a monotonous way. Perhaps you have suffered from the "death by bullet points" syndrome: bullets made the presentation boring and did not capture the attention of the audience. They aren't as vivid or memorable as visual charts and graphs, or as single words or numbers on one slide, and do not lend themselves to creating a "wow!" factor, as in Steve Jobs's compelling Apple product presentations that you can find online, e.g.: http://www.youtube.com/watch?v=Z0jIpSCndtw .

Online audiences are easy to lose within the first few minutes of a presentation, so the challenge is to engage them in a way that will allow them to remember the main key points (audience takeaway). Below are some simple ways to enhance your presentations — and to guide your students in enhancing their presentations of their projects in order to increase audience takeaway:

a. Have clear objectives.

It is essential for the presenter(s) to have their objectives in mind before they begin their presentation. They need to think about why they are offering their presentation and what the audience is supposed to gain from the experience. What do you want the audience to take away? From there, you can have a clear starting point, as well as a clear direction in which to take your audience. Setting the outcomes of your presentation will help you reverse-engineer it.. You will gain a clear focus on what needs to be included in the presentation and what needs to be omitted. Clarity of objectives will also boost the audience's engagement and will give them a sense of purpose. A presentation with clear objectives is essential for the teacher, in the case where the teacher needs to lecture their students or provide perspectives on course content, just as it is essential for learners who need to present their projects in a synchronous or asynchronous manner to fellow learners and who wish to obtain high marks.

b.   *Start with the essential information first.*

As the presenter(s) will have the attention of their audience at the start of their presentation, they can use to advantage the reverse pyramid principle: clearly stating the point of the lecture, lesson, or project presentation first. This will allow the audience to understand what they need to pay attention to and what they should take away from the presentation. It might sound a little strange to present the most important information first, but when the presenter establishes objectives and gets to the point of their presentation right away, the audience is clearly orientated and more likely to retain what the presenter considers to be important. Following up core statements with examples and supporting details adds to the audience's sensitivity to and understanding of the main points, and at the end of the presentation audience orientation and take-away can be reinforced with a re-statement of objectives and main information. This way the presenter will follow a natural attention cycle and give the most crucial material at the peaks of learner receptivity. Opening a discussion board on which comments and questions concerning the presentation — lecture, lesson, project presentation, etc. — can be aired is a necessary step in relating learning to the personal concerns and experience of the audience and in creating an opportunity for the presenter(s) to deepen their own sensitivity to and understanding of the issues in question (see below part e. Create interaction).

c.   Use visualization.

If the presenter decides to use PowerPoint presentations, they need to think about the content of each slide and how its visual content is communicating the important information. The presenter must consider the main points they want to convey and then decide if they need to add images to enhance the presentation, i.e., pictures, diagrams, etc. For example, think about a lecture in which you aim to teach the conversion of carbohydrates to energy in cells. Not only is it helpful to describe the process, but also a diagram of what this process looks like, how it works, and where the cycle begins again will allow students to grasp your perspective of core concepts. Clearly diagramming each stage will ensure a clear and memorable explanation of the complexities of the conversion process. You may also want to use the principle of "cognitive dissonance" where images on the slide at first do not seem to relate to one another. This will keep your audience's attention active because they will try to guess the missing information until you eventually make the connection between the pictures clear.

Compare the slides below. Which one do you think your audience will remember?

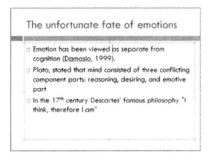

d.   Remember your audience's needs.

In any presentation, academic or otherwise, the presenter(s) needs to remember that their audience is wondering, "What's in it for me?" Prior to giving a lecture or presenting a project, it is advisable for the presenter(s) to learn as much as they can about their audience to ensure they are addressing their needs, as well as becoming a part of a dialogue, rather than just speaking at the audience. By understanding and acknowledging the audience's needs, the presenter(s) can create content that is valuable to them and in turn ensure their engagement. Presenting core concepts as being of great relevance to their audience is crucial.

e.   Create interaction.

While we are all familiar with passive presentations where the presenter believes that knowledge goes one way — from the lecturer or student presenter to the audience (most lectures and presentations are still structured this way) — they are not typically effective. This is because this kind of presentation is an impoverished form of knowledge generation, in which the members of the audience are unable to engage in concept formation, or relate ideas to their own experience, through discussions in which meaning is negotiated with the presenter and fellow participants. Instead of this one-way approach, let your students become a part of the presentation, co-creating the content through discussion so that it allows them to stay engaged. You can create interaction during your lectures in a variety of ways. Some strategies for you—and your students in their presentations — include the following:

- Show that you have an open mind by asking your audience open-ended questions.
- Show a genuine interest in their answers and probe their reasoning.
- Show early on that you realize that what you are claiming to be the case is just your perspective and can change through exposure to legitimate ideas.
- Encourage the audience to set the agenda.
- Propose key issues to resolve, or puzzles that encourage the audience to become active.
- Show an interest in audience perspectives: ask if there are any other issues that need addressing.
- Invite your students to demonstrate a point through personal examples or role play (if appropriate).
- Play with your audience, putting up a slide or making a comment that seems irrelevant, and asking if there is any connection to the current discussion.

When you address the audience directly, you will create a more exciting presentation where the audience feels they have a say in what is being presented. Remember that an audience generally has an attention span of about twenty minutes, so make sure that you and your students or trainees know about the importance of creating breaks (i.e. actual breaks, or soft breaks like puzzles, games, and surveys) in your presentation time if your lecture or presentation is longer than twenty to twenty-five minutes.

f. Practice your presentation skills.

The more you practice your presentation skills, the more polished you will appear. When the presenter is comfortable speaking in front of the audience, the audience is more willing to trust the information being presented, and it will ensure that you are delivering the material in an effective way. Here are some ways to practice your presentation:

- Videotape your online presentation. Look at it through the audience's eyes.
- Take a training course if possible. If not, watch other presenters that inspire you. Write down all the strategies that make them effective. Try to adapt them in your personal presentation.
- Ask for feedback from others. Sometimes your family and friends are your best critics. Ask them to give you a true opinion of your lecture. Make them list positive and negative features of your presentation.
- Keep practicing and reflecting. There is no magic formula for becoming a great presenter. Practice is the number-one requirement for polishing your skills. Thinking about what worked and what needs to work better next time will help you to perfect your presentations.

g. Use the right technology.

While PowerPoint is one beneficial tool for presentations, it is certainly not the only tool. Think instead about the material you want to present and how it can be shown in the most effective way. Slides may not be effective in some cases, while visual aids may be essential in others. Mind-mapping software such as freemind.sourceforge.net/ can be used to present information in a more interactive way. Consider the presentation content and then use media that supports the content, rather than hinders it.

h. Ask for feedback.

Though you may not want to know how your presentation went and let students express their opinion of your presentation content, feedback is essential for improving your skills. Ask your students to give you informal feedback after your presentation — perhaps on the continuous improvement "How can we do better?" discussion board set aside for student suggestions on the course and its teaching. This will help you perfect your delivery the next time you present.

i. Follow up.

After your presentation is over, it is a good idea to check in with the audience to see what they have remembered and retained. Many studies cite the idea that humans forget about 75 percent of what they have learned within twenty-four hours, but with effective presentations particularly those that have invited audience participation and discussion — you can ensure this is not the case with your students.

j. Deliver it well.

Just as important as what you say during a presentation is how you say it. Think about the last time you listened to a monotonous speech. Do you remember what was said? Now remember an inspiring speaker. How did she deliver her presentation? Did she emphasize certain words? Speed up and slow down at certain points? Create pauses? Ask thought-provoking questions? Leave you feeling that you had gained important new insights that enhanced your sensitivity to and understanding of issues important to your life?

Here are some ideas on how you — and your students in presenting their work — might improve your presentation delivery, especially during video-conferencing:

- Connect emotionally. Ask the audience what they are curious about, what interests them, and try to understand and articulate their needs. Ask if anyone has experienced what you are talking about. Ask if you have missed anything. Challenge them with an extreme example. Call into question common-sense notions. Evoke strong emotions in your audience by presenting an idea that seems counterintuitive, an attention-grabbing question, an image, a short video.

- Be scholarly and receptive. State sincerely that you understand that you are giving a perspective only and are curious to learn yourself.

- Follow the 10-20-30 rule. Guy Kawasaki from Apple says that following the 10-20-30 rule is the best advice for PowerPoint and slide presentations. You should have no more than 10 slides that last no more than 20 minutes and with text no less than 30 point size.

- Make eye contact. Try to make eye contact with the webcam during both synchronous and recorded lectures to ensure engagement.

- Speak slowly. It's natural for you to speak more quickly when you're nervous, so make a concerted effort to speak slowly during presentations.

- Have a short summary. Try to have a fifteen-word summary of your content before you begin. If your summary is longer, try to condense it.
- Don't read your presentation. While it might be tempting to read your presentation, this can make your delivery distracting as the audience may not see you as having confidence in what you're sharing.
- Offer stories. Whenever possible, offer stories to support your information. This will help to keep the audience interested in what you are sharing.
- Project your voice. Try to speak loudly and clearly so that everyone can hear you. Especially online, you need to make sure your words can be heard.
- Stall during questions. When you are not sure how to answer a question, or you need time to think about the answer, use phrases like "That's a good question" or "I'm glad you asked that" to buy yourself time to think. If you don't know the answer, admit that you do not have the answer at that moment and get back with the response after the presentation.
- Use gestures only when you need to make a point, and do so naturally.
- Breathe. Instead of saying "uh" or other filler words, take a moment to breathe. This will make you look more confident while giving you a moment to collect your thoughts.
- Arrive early for a synchronous lecture. This will ensure that you're not rushed and that you can test your equipment, solving any problems before the audience arrives.

- Practice. It can't be stated enough that you need to practice before you present.
- Think about what you would want if you were in the audience. Put yourself in the shoes of the people in your audience and think about what your presentation needs to include in order to be effective and beneficial.
- Have fun. While the subject matter may not be exciting to some, you should show your interest in it and have fun when you present it. This attitude will be infectious.
- Challenge your audience. Ask questions that make your audience members rethink their perceptions; a revelation can produce a "wow!" moment that the audience won't soon forget.
- Apologize when you're wrong. If you are incorrect, then apologize, but do not apologize for being nervous, as this will cause the audience to see nervousness that they might not have noticed before.

Remember: the more presentations you give, the easier they will become!

Secret #3: Writing for Web-Based Context

While presentations are certainly a key tool in educating online, they are not the only tool to create content that increases students' performance. Writing effectively for the web is another skill you need to develop. Just as audiences in presentations can become bored by the content when not presented well, when writing for the web, your words need to be presented effectively. You need to be clear about what you want your students to remember — to take away — before you post anything on the web, and you also need to be aware of your audience's areas of interest. When your writing is effective — when it is clear, concise, and relevant, containing concrete examples and humor — students will be able to understand important information more easily. When your students prepare small or large postings or project texts for the course, they will be able to draw upon your example to express their production effectively and therefore perform at a higher level.

It is important is to remember that online writing is different from traditional writing. You might have to overcome resistance to changing your style, because over many years you have developed a face-to-face style of which you are proud. However, when writing online content, it is very important to adapt your style to the psychology of this educational context. Dr. Nielsen has graciously allowed us to share his findings on this topic in this book. According to Nielsen & Pernice (2010), most people who read information online will only read about 20 percent of the material, often only scanning the pages for the information that pertains to their concerns. Despite the fact that more people have been using the Internet in recent years, this behavior has remained consistent.

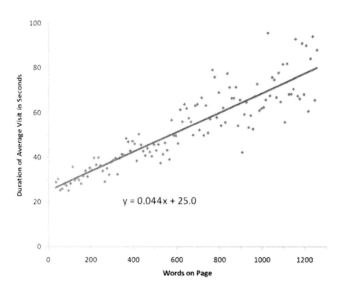

(Source: http://www.useit.com/)

The above picture demonstrates the average time users spend on pages with different word counts. According to Nielsen, while readers do spend more time on pages with more content, they only add 4.4 seconds for every additional one hundred words! Many people who look at information online will use the back button, which is something you need to keep in mind when writing online. Attention spans are shorter in the digital world, with online studies of reading behavior showing that students are less likely to read longer pages of text. In fact, studies have also shown that even with the required reading material, only about 10 percent of students will actually complete the reading assignments in full. What is clear from Nielsen's extensive research is that students will spend time reviewing the navigation of a page, but they may not spend as much time reviewing the actual content. Nielsen tried to calculate the maximum amount of text users could read during an average visit to pages with different word counts, which is reflected in the picture below.

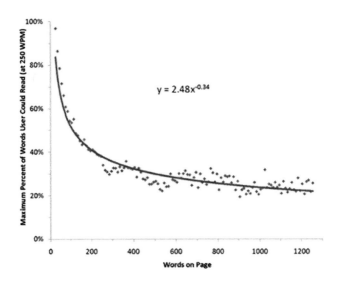

$$y = 2.48x^{-0.34}$$

As we can see, the percentage of read material rapidly declines as the word count increases. Nielsen concludes that on average users read only half the information on those pages with 111 words or less, while they read about 20 percent of all information on pages with higher word count. These findings add up to a need for shorter word counts, rather than the longer pages of content that are so common in academia. Now, we are not encouraging you to shorten the assignments that you set for your trainees or students. What we suggest is that if you require a long reading, make it printable. When you create other content that is posted on your class site, keep in mind the following psychological findings:

a. Many online readers will only focus on the first eleven characters of a page, and then focus on certain parts of a page on the left side of a page and lists.

b. Lists are often read completely as they offer truncated pieces of information and direction for the reader. Lists occur in a variety of places:

   • assignment listings
   • archives

- headlines
- news items
- table of content listings
- numbered/bulleted lists
- FAQs

Even in these lists, most readers will only skim the first two words of the listed item to see if it contains the information they need.

c. When adding links to a web page, which can be helpful in directing the reader, you will need to make sure they are short and to the point:
- Use simple, plain language.
- Be specific in terminology.
- Use conventions for naming common features.
- Think about action-oriented items.

Links that don't get clicked as often are those that

- use generic wordings;
- offer made-up words;
- place the useful information at the end of the link's name.

The key with links is to make sure they are

- not misleading;
- clearly differentiated from the navigation links;
- predictive for the user: the links you include need to ensure the reader understands their usefulness for their query.

d. In addition to links, remember that how a reader reads a page can impact their understanding and their engagement for longer periods of time. Nielsen suggests that an F-shaped pattern has been shown to be the most effective for readers, as this is their natural reading pattern online. F-shape stands for "fast" and for the two horizontal stripes followed by the vertical stripe of reading. This means that

- users read the top first, often the top bar content;
- users read below the top bar content to get a sense of the page;
- users review the left-side menu.

The picture below demonstrates this pattern:

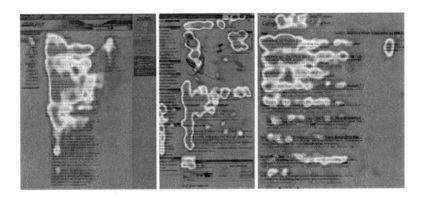

Heatmap images that demonstrate F-shape pattern of reading online texts

The picture above reflects heatmaps from user eye-tracking studies of three websites. The red colors show the most popular parts of the content, the yellow areas reflect fewer views, the blue areas are the least viewed, while the gray areas did not attract any eye fixations. While this pattern does not match the reading patterns of all users, knowing where the reader will look for information can help you in writing and designing the web content of your online class. If you are not aware of the F-shaped pattern, this can lead to troubles with web page use as readers will not read the content thoroughly and leave out most important information. Therefore, since readers will not read your content thoroughly, you should state the most important information in the first two paragraphs and start subheads, paragraphs, and bulleted points with the information-carrying words that will be placed within the F-shape.

About Dr. Jacob Nielsen

Jakob Nielsen, PhD (www.useit.com) is a principal of Nielsen Norman Group (www.nngroup.com). He is the founder of the "discount usability engineering" movement, which emphasizes fast and efficient methods for improving the quality of user interfaces. Nielsen, noted as "the world's leading expert on web usability" by U.S. News and World Report and "the next best thing to a true time machine" by USA Today, is the author of the bestselling book Designing Web Usability: The Practice of Simplicity (1999), which has sold more than a quarter of a million copies in twenty-two languages. His other books include Hypertext and Hypermedia (1990), Usability Engineering (1993), Usability Inspection Methods (1994), International User Interfaces (1996), Homepage Usability: 50 Websites Deconstructed (2001), Prioritizing Web Usability (2006), and Eyetracking Web Usability (2009). Nielsen's Alertbox column on web usability has been published on the Internet since 1995 and currently has about 200,000 readers. From 1994 to 1998, Nielsen was a Sun Microsystems Distinguished Engineer. His previous affiliations include Bell Communications Research, the Technical University of Denmark, and the IBM User Interface Institute. He holds seventy-nine US patents, mainly on ways of making the Internet easier to use.

Secret #4: Assessing Students' Learning

Assessing your students is a necessary tool in gauging the learning and the performance of your students. By finding out how students are doing, you can ensure they are on the right track, or you can determine when you need to step in. By assessing students, you can also provide feedback that can challenge them and encourage them to deepen their learning. Because online learning can be challenging in offering real-time feedback, online assessment can be a topic for a separate book. However, here we will briefly describe various types of assessment tools that you can use in your distance learning classroom.

a. Fixed-Choice Tests

When you offer tests online, you can immediately determine whether the students have gained the expected knowledge from lessons.

These tests include the following:

- true/false
- multiple-choice

In these tests, there is one right answer to the question, helping to instantly see if the student is on the right track. At the same time, you need to keep in mind that these tests can also have results based on guessing by students, as opposed to actual recognition of the right answers.

Of these two fixed-choice tests, multiple-choice tests offer a stronger assessment of student performance. Not only can multiple-choice tests help to assess the basic knowledge of students, but they can also help to assess more complicated lessons and how students have processed the information. The automatic scoring offers immediate feedback after students take the multiple-choice tests, so you can quickly determine the success of a course or lesson. You can also include media with your multiple-choice tests when you use certain programs.

Novo: Wow! I think I'll use multiple-choice tests for all of my assessments. I know what my students need to know and marking is quick and easy.

Lauri: Multiple-choice tests limit students' learning to what the teacher knows, which we all know is not much in any subject area these days. Rather than passively absorb someone else's viewpoint, students need to research, discuss, and produce — particularly, they need to find information relevant to their own experience and what is new in the field of inquiry. For this and other reasons, multiple-choice tests have limitations: they can be ambiguous if poorly written, if they contain inadequate contextual information, test memory rather than how learning might be applied to issues, contain no social validation of responses, do not emerge from a learner's interests, and do not reveal the reasoning behind responses. As these limitations greatly reduce the usefulness of multiple-choice tests for learners and teachers alike, individual or group project work, rather than multiple choice, is preferable for major assessments.

Some helpful resources for creating multiple-choice tests, web course development, and automatic grading include the following:

- Blackboard: www.blackboard.com
- Moodle: http://moodle.org/
- IntraLearn: www.intralearn.com
- KnowledgeLinx: www.knowledgelinx.net
- Learning Space: www.lotus.com/home.nsf/tabs/learnspace
- Prometheus: www.prometheus.com/
- Quiz Book: www.doversw.com/quizbook.htm
- Quiz Factory & Quiz Rocket: www.learningware.com
- QuizMaker: www.attotron.com/pub/Quizmaker.html

- ToolBook/Assistant: www.click2learn.com
- TopClass: www.wbtsystems.com

b.   *Short Answers and Essay Questions*

Online educators will often avoid using short answer and essay assessments with students, as they can be difficult to grade when class sizes are large. However, short answer and essay assessments provide for greater insight into student competence and thinking processes. To help the problem of grading such questions, you might use the following:

- Computer-graded essays. Software is now being used for advanced tests, including the GMAT, with a computer and a human grader both looking at the text to assess the content.
- Third-party assessments. You can also look into third parties who will use a rubric to evaluate the content of the short answer and essay tests. With at least two evaluators, the scoring becomes more reliable.

Additional software resources for short answer and essay tests include the following:

- CyberProf: www.howhy.com/home
- Mallard: www.cen.uiuc.edu/Mallard/Overview/
- Blackboard: www.blackboard.com

Note: Even if you use technology to grade your students' short answers, you will still need to double check computer-based responses before you come up with the final grade for the assignment.

Writing a detailed essay marking sheet can help you to think clearly about what you value in terms of thinking processes and content outcomes. A marking sheet can help you to be fair in assessing essays, and can show students clearly where they need to improve.

You can copy and paste a marking sheet to word.doc essays. In-text comments on word.doc essays can be in the form of comment balloons, in which you can put generic or original comments designed to help the learner to improve their essay writing or their thinking in the subject area, and thus improve their future performance. Ending all comments with a question mark shows that you are not being categorical, but are making a suggestion of which the learner can judge the relevance. Asking a question is more likely to engage the learner in a reflection on their work. Setting a small essay at the beginning of the course, perhaps offering the question up for negotiation and accepting valid adjustments, allows for comments on essay structure, the stating of an argument, the development of the argument, referencing quality and procedures, and the construction of a conclusion to be given as feedback before a major essay is written.

c. Performance Tasks

Many online educators are interested in teaching at the same time as students are working on assessment tasks that will demonstrate their learning as applied to important issues relevant to the course. By setting performance tasks such as project work or essay writing, both of these goals can be reached. Performance tasks can be extensive, so assigning these to groups of students, as opposed to individuals, allows for sharing the workload, intersubjective validation of ideas, and a broader inquiry in the subject area.

Some tips for creating effective performance tasks include encouraging the following:

- E-delivery of assignments. Allow students to deliver assignments via e-mail, wiki, or other electronic means. Have students contact each other about the assignments, with the permission of the students to release their contact information. Students' reporting back to other students in order to get constructive feedback on individual or group work can be organized early on, when tasks are negotiated and allocated.

- Contacting teachers. Encourage students to reach out to teachers over e-mail or other means if they have questions or concerns.

- Chat rooms. Use ICQ technology so that students can talk in real time with each other whenever possible.

- Class website. Have a central class website where students can access course information at any time.

- Electronic bulletin boards. Offer a place where students can post questions to the entire class or where you can post announcements for everyone to review. For a more substantial discussion, post articles or links to videos from reputable sources that can enhance sensitivity to and understanding of issues relevant to assessment questions and core course concerns.

- List serve. Sign up for a list serve where a message can be e-mailed to everyone in the class at once, and students can use this service to e-mail their classmates.

- Groupware. When students may need to see graphics or a writing space at the same time, Groupware can help to create this learning environment.
- Videoconferencing. With videoconferencing, students can see each other during tasks.

Remember that the teacher does not have to be the only person who gives an opinion that counts toward an assessment of a learner's work. Projects and essays can also be marked by the teacher, and the student(s) who have produced the piece of work, and/or their classmates. A student or project team can negotiate evaluation criteria with the teacher at the inception of their project, and can report back to their classmates for feedback — "What have we done and what have we still got to do?" — during the construction of their projects. A student or project team can mark their own work, according to their detailed and personalized marking sheet that they have negotiated with the teacher, and make their marked work available for classmates and the teacher to see and discuss. Their classmates can also mark the work in question, and the teacher as well. The teacher can then look at the authors' mark and the classmates' mark, and take these into account when awarding a final mark. This process broadens the learning experience and encourages scholarly reflection and interaction, and excellence of work.

d. Portfolios and Journals

Additional tools for assessment that online educators can utilize are portfolios and journals. These are tools that are student-created, including photos, videos, and graphics that pertain to certain lessons, or to students' experience while working on a group project. For example, a diary can deal with students' insights concerning their own and others' contributions to a group project, or with how students feel they are progressing. There are also e-portfolios online, see http://www.eportfolio.org/

e. Teacher, Self and Peer Evaluation

Another type of assessment is various forms of evaluation. You can ask students to provide evaluation of your work using a rubric that will demonstrate to you where you can improve. You can also encourage student self and peer evaluations. Students can negotiate the evaluation criteria and then mark each other's (or their own) work. When the teacher grades a student's work, she can take self and peer marks into account.

Secret #5: Gamification

Education is often seen as a practice of memorization by rote learning, which is an impoverished form of learning that involves the teacher's colonization of the learner with her ideas and perspectives, presented uncritically as objective "facts," ignoring the learner's interests, opinions, growth toward independence, need to negotiate meaning, and need to validate his point of view through discussion, enjoyment in the learning process, and reasons for engaging in the learning process, all of which mean that the student's potential learning is limited by this approach. Educational games can provide an immediate release from a traditional rote or knowledge-transfer learning experience, as they develop capability (solution-based learning) rather than competence ("fact"-based learning). Games have a textuality that is appealing to students and conducive to an intersubjective learning context. They provide an exciting and effective learning opportunity that involves learners' solving real-life problems collaboratively. They can be the center-piece of a rich learning process.

The core educative interest of games is that they require the reason-ing of strategy individually or collectively, which is conducive to discussion and argument, and thus an intersubjective learning process. Teams can play against teams, or individuals against their classmates. The teacher can inter-rupt the game at any time to ask for an explanation of past strategy or an elucidation of strategic options or expected outcomes. A teacher will choose a game that deals with skills or issues that are relevant to the subject area being explored in the learning process, and the educative assumption is that the playing of the game will engage students in an analysis of important concerns and possible approaches to dealing with them, with the possibility of integrating current learning from course materials in the formulation of solutions. The notion of play invites student engagement because of its ele-ments of creative thinking, self-directed learning, social context, collabora-tion, competition, and ensuing enjoyment, which can in turn lead to more investment and performance in a course. As it is expected that some will win and some will lose, and that there is an element of chance, failure is not necessarily as painful an experience as, for example, failing a test can be. Games can be sources of both formative and summative assessment, and can reveal common interests and engender mutual appreciation across social stratifications.

Some examples of online educational games include the following:

- Boom Box. This tool offers students the chance to solve physics-based puzzles. With numerous levels of challenges and different multiplayer levels, students are constantly learning more about the material.

- Fan Fiction. Instead of approaching literary works from the content alone, students can be encouraged to write supplementary fictional works, based on what they know about the characters. By placing the characters in new environments, it can help students understand the characters on a more advanced level.

Part 4: Three Secrets of Creating Enjoyment Online

Do you have a love-hate relationship with technology? Have you ever prepared a class or a training session that took hours to develop, only to find out on the day that the network was down? Have you ever spent ages recording a video, only to realize afterwards that your sound did not work? Have you ever sat down to correct students' papers and got sucked into looking at e-mails and browsing content? Have you ever spent your entire day without leaving your house, or even days, perhaps never changing out of your pajamas, feeling that your life was wasting away? We have all been in situations like this. While technology is designed to make our lives easier, it can also bring a lot of frustration to anyone's teaching or training experience.

With the rapid advancement of technology over the past two decades, online learning has grown enormously and is only continuing to grow. However, few tactics and strategies have been developed to help us survive this cyber jungle and start enjoying our new educational context. We dream about having a flexible schedule and working from home, but when we actually get an online teaching position we complain that we become slaves to the computer and that we spend more time working than in a regular office job. How can we enjoy the advantages of the online context?

Being happy and joyful online is an important quality of a teacher, but it is also a path filled with sacrifice and obstacles. As teachers we are results-oriented. Certainly, we want our students to learn and need to think about our future goals and the outcomes of our teaching. However, in order to truly enjoy our online teaching experience, we also need to relish the process of teaching itself in its entirety. Education counselor Dr. Wayne Dyer reminds us that "When you dance, your purpose is not to get to a certain place on the floor. It's to enjoy each step along the way." Instead, most of us feel overwhelmed and overworked during the process and do not allow ourselves the time to take pleasure in what is rewarding. As a result we show less engagement and are less inspiring to others. When we are content with our job, we communicate this enjoyment and enthusiasm to our students. We become more engaged, productive, perceptive, and receptive. We have a more positive attitude toward difficulties that arise during our online experience. Becoming happy with our job is not a selfish act; we owe it to ourselves, to our students, and to everyone whose life we affect.

No one teaches you how to be happy online. This subject is not included in your distance learning teacher preparation program — if you are lucky enough to have had one. In this section, we will address some strategies that will raise your level of enjoyment in the online context and will help you to create the lifestyle that you desire. This list of strategies is not exhaustive. Nevertheless, we believe that if you implement these three secrets alone, the quality of your online experience will increase dramatically.

Secret #1: Managing Your Workload

Tool 1: Shifting the Locus of Control

Distance learning cannot be approached in the same way as in a face-to-face context. It involves different modes of connection, communication, perception, and interpretation, and thus requires a different pedagogy. In order to enjoy online teaching, the teaching approach needs to be adapted to that context in terms of both pedagogy and the way a teacher relates to her students or trainees. If a teacher tries to approach distance learning with the same repertoire of tools that she uses in a traditional classroom, she will most probably feel frustrated, burned out, and ineffective in this new educational environment. According to Reeves (2002), "Good online learning should require more than a mere shift from one medium to another. Instructional methods must be enhanced to take advantage of the affordances of technology." Moreover, as we have discussed earlier, the teacher needs to take her students beyond instruction toward construction and social validation: toward pieces of work that are the fruit of research and discussions emanating from reporting progress back to classmates, that may involve group collaboration, that are relevant to students' or trainees' interests and ambitions, and that might include well-founded ideas the teacher has never heard of. The online context provides an opportunity for teachers to create a student-centered classroom, where the locus of control shifts from the teacher to the student.

The role of the teacher thus becomes different online than in a face-to-face context. In the traditional environment the importance of a student-centered approach has been recognized since the 1970s. However, in creating the conditions in which learners can be self-directed and thrive in their autonomy online, the locus of control has to shift even more to the student and away from the teacher. Online teachers have "the responsibility of keeping discussions on track, contributing special knowledge and insights, weaving together various discussion threads and course components, and maintaining group harmony" (Berge, 1995). The teacher is also no longer the provider of information or an initiator of classroom activities. Therefore, online learning is not only student-centered, but also student-driven. The online teacher stops being a separate entity in the classroom. She becomes a contributing member of a team, who does not necessarily have control of the learning environment, as students are no longer dependent on the teacher alone for knowledge, having a variety of resources available at their finger-tips. In creating with her students a climate in which they can move toward autonomy, she becomes a resource, a guide, and a negotiator, working with students to orientate their projects toward their interests and ambitions, put-ting the focus, value, and deadline of each piece of work to be completed in a course up for discussion — and anything else a student or trainee might wish to adapt to their particular needs.

So what is the purpose of the teacher online? As Muirhead (2001) says, the traditional role of teachers has shifted from information-transmitters to guides who create meaningful learner-centered experiences in which students construct their own understanding of reality. Instead of filling your participants up with knowledge, you go on a journey of discov-ery with them, fostering discussion concerning the value and relevance of what is found. As this journey is full of uncertainty and risk, due to the need for learners to be self-directed, initiate research and develop projects, expose work to peers for criticism, and even manage collaboration with others, the teacher has to create a climate in which the learner feels supported and secure and free to explore. Accordingly, an online teacher is also responsible for maintaining an interrelational climate in which building teacher-learner relationships is of great importance. In the next chapter we will discuss in detail how to create with your students an interrelational climate conducive to student engagement, autonomy, performance and enjoyment. For now, we would like to invite you to consider this new role that you have in your distance classroom and think about the ways to re-assign your time and energy from providing information to guiding, from teaching to facilitating.

Many studies suggest that the constructivist model of teaching works best for the online environment. According to this model, people are constantly trying to make sense of the world around them based on their previous experience. "A person's processes are psychologically channelized by the ways in which he anticipates events" (Kelly 1955, p. 46). Kelly (1955) believed that we anticipate events by "construing their replications" (p. 50), which means that we continually give meaning to events through our interpretation of them. Each individual creates her meaning differently and continually re-negotiates his "reality" through conversation with others. Consequently, the learning process requires both an individual and a social dimension. Learners inquire into an area of interest and construct meaning in response to texts and conversations with other students and the teacher, as they build up a response or solution to the focus questions. The focus of inquiry provides the context for the learners to investigate, socially validate, and apply their knowledge and to take ownership of their learning. Instead of giving the answer and transmitting the knowledge, the teacher can start by asking guiding questions and taking a genuine interest in her students' perspectives, avoiding where possible the notion of right and wrong answers. The teacher needs to develop an online learning community where students build knowledge together with their peers and their teacher. All members of the learning community support each other intellectually and emotionally and depend on each other to achieve the learning outcomes for the course. According to Smith (2005), building an online community is so important that without it there is no online course.

In the next chapter we will discuss the role of the teacher in more detail. What we want you to take away from this section is that you do not need to do absolutely everything in your online course. Step back, give up complete control, give up the need to be everything for everyone, and create the conditions for your students and trainees to be self-directed, socially connected, and bring their pieces of work to fruition in line with their interests. Accordingly, a successful online teacher needs to find answers to the following questions: How can you build true connection with your students? How can you create an environment of trust and care? How can you allow your students to be on their personal quest of knowledge, yet remind them that you are there to help them? The answers will re-define your role as an online teacher. When you adopt this new role, the quality of your students' learning experience, including their confidence to be self-directed, will increase and your time management will improve immensely.

Tool # 2: Setting Your Own Schedule

In order to truly enjoy your online experience, to avoid being overwhelmed, and to develop a balance between work and personal life, it is important to implement effective time management strategies. The best way to become a happy online teacher is to design your ideal schedule first and then work backwards to fit all your work into this pre-defined day. How many hours a day would you be willing to work in order to still have time for yourself and your family? Do you want to work on weekends or holidays? Each of us has a different understanding of an ideal work schedule. Therefore, all you need to do is to determine what would make you happy and then reverse-engineer your day. Sounds like it is too good to be true? Not really. Setting your perfect schedule requires a lot of self-discipline and also an ability to say no to other obligations or tasks, and even at times turn people down who are not contributing to this ideal lifestyle.

Setting up your ideal schedule will help you start living according to your priorities. Once you identify the activities that you love and people that you want to spend time with, and set up your perfect working day, you will consciously invite only those priorities into your day, leaving no room for anything else. Tim Ferris, an author of best-selling The 4-Hour Work Week, uses Parkinson's Law to make his key point. According to this law, more time does not mean more results. If we identify most important tasks and assign time limits for their completion, we will be surprised at how quickly our brains "regroups" and how much more productive we become. A strategy for successful time management is thus organizing your day in "time chunks." If you determine that you need, say, three hours to correct students' work, you will make sure to eliminate all distractions and concentrate on that task for that amount of time. You will discover that you actually do not need an entire day for this activity — something you would be doing if you did not set time limits.

When you set your own schedule and break your day into blocks, you will see a number of positive consequences. You will realize that your productivity increases, you will eliminate time wasters and you will also teach other people how to treat you. For example, you can let your students know that you will answer their e-mails within twenty-four hours but not every ten minutes. Limiting your time might sound counterintuitive as we are conditioned to see the ability to juggle several activities at once as a positive feature. Nevertheless, when you only focus on your priorities and dedicate specific time in your schedule to each of them, you will be giving them more attention and you will achieve more results, while being able to have time for yourself and your family. This strategy works well for any job environment, but it is especially powerful for teaching online as you can create the lifestyle of your dreams with its help. There is only one condition to this dream: you must be in charge of setting up your day so it reflects your dream job and nothing violates or detracts from it.

Secret #2 Managing Your Online Classroom

Tool 1: Conflict Resolution

Do you remember a time when a seemingly unimportant issue got blown out of proportion online and became a source of major conflict? As we have said before, the online environment is extremely conducive to heightened emotional responses, and your feelings and dispositions are transparent to others. It is also a potentially volatile environment that can turn a casually thrown word into an angry exchange. Why does cyberspace ignite so many conflicts and misunderstandings?

Certainly, the impersonal nature of online interactions makes this context difficult to handle. Because of the lack of visual cues (gestures and facial expressions) and auditory support (such as tone of voice or intonations), there is much more room left for misunderstanding online than in a traditional setting. Being blind to the physical expressions of other people, which are usually responsible for 80 percent of our total understanding, we create meanings in our head based on limited information. Since we serve as interpreters of someone else's intentions, our personal mood or mindset plays a huge role in our understanding of the messages that we receive. Therefore it is important to be aware of a variety of psychological processes that we use when we communicate in this cyber jungle, and draw upon this knowledge to adjust our reactions to others when we interact online.

a. Online Projections

Certainly, for the majority of us, the way we read someone's e-mails or online messages is the only way they can be read. Unfortunately, that is far from the truth. Often the way we interpret someone's words reflects our personal inner world, our feelings, motivations (or the lack of them), and our personal self-judgment. Using the language of psychologists, we are "projecting" our expectations, needs, and feelings onto other people. Because an online context is deprived of the physical manifestations of someone else's intentions, it reflects our own intentions, problems, insecurities, or concerns. It functions like a large mirror that can show us how WE feel at a particular moment.

How do we acquire such projections? Some people call it "baggage" and some, a "personal story"; the labels do not really matter here. What is important is that most of us carry a collection of situations and experiences that have happened in our past, a summary of the way we have been treated or memories of the models of behavior that we inherited from the authority figures in our lives who taught us how to act, see ourselves, cope with difficult situations, and enjoy life. These experiences are so firmly engraved in our minds that we often react on autopilot, and do not have time to stop and think that our response is actually connected to our past and not to the present situation. Have you ever read an e-mail when you were tired or frustrated and been insulted by it, only to find yourself reading the same e-mail later on, when you were in good spirits, and not finding anything negative in it? Have you ever shared a written note that you had found offensive with your close friend or spouse, but instead of finding their total support you were shocked and even upset at their failure to see the situation through your eyes? Certainly, there are occasional situations when someone purposefully wants to criticize or disrespect us, but they are rare. In the majority of situations it is more likely that it is our own projections that hurt and insult us, and remembering this will help you to avoid many negative situations in your distance learning classroom and increase your enjoyment of your online experience.

Novo: I've just received an e-mail that says that I need to be more "cool" in my responses online. That's outrageous! What an insult! I'm going to write back straight away and give them a piece of my mind.

Lauri: Is that being cool? It's better to take ten deep breaths, leave the e-mails, and come back to it later on. When you answer an email online, never be defensive; give the person the benefit of the doubt and reply as if you were not being attacked in any way. Here is an opportunity to use your sense of humor and to say something like, "Thanks for your e-mail. Sorry if the pressure's showing — yes, I could have been more cool. From now on, Zen is my middle name." If this doesn't settle things down immediately, pick up the phone, and call them.

b. Disinhibition Effect

Another interesting psychological phenomenon that happens online and that has been described by Dr. John Suler is a "disinhibition effect," according to which humans express themselves in a freer way online than in person. "It's well known," says Suler (2002), "that people say and do things in cyberspace that they wouldn't ordinarily say or do in the face-to-face world. They loosen up, feel more uninhibited, express themselves more openly. Researchers call this the 'disinhibition effect.' It's a double-edged sword. Sometimes people share personal things about themselves; they reveal secret emotions, fears, wishes. Or they show unusual acts of kindness and generosity. On the other hand, the disinhibition effect may not be so benign. Out spills rude language and harsh criticisms, anger, hatred, even threats" (Suler, 2002). According to Suler, there are several reasons for the disinhibition effect that arise from the very nature of online interactions.

Anonymity. Since it is possible to "hide behind the screen" online and even accept a different identity, it is easier to say whatever you feel and not worry that someone might catch you.

Invisibility. Because no one sees your facial expressions, or the way you look or talk, and cannot give you a disapproving frown or any other expression, you can feel "safe" to say what you really feel online.

Delayed response. Since it is possible to post online 24/7 and participate in a conversation, even when your audience is not yet there, you can share your feelings whenever you want to, without worrying about someone else's immediate reaction. If you like, you can even share your deepest fears or concerns and never come back to the conversation thread, avoiding ANY type of reactions from your audience, performing so-called emotional hit and run.

Status defusing. Since in a face-to-face context you might feel reluctant to express negative emotions towards your superior or other "authority" figures (your relatives, parents, etc.), all statuses seem to dissolve online.

Multiplied emotions. Since the online environment tends to make emotions and communication styles even more exaggerated, you might find yourself reacting with much more strength online than in a face-to-face context.

Knowledge of these psychological processes that are particular to the online environment is crucial in order to create a peaceful, welcoming, and joyful experience online. However, knowledge of these phenomena is not enough. You need to know HOW to navigate through the emotional minefield that is produced by cyberspace. Specifically for this purpose, we have conducted an interview with a specialist in conflict resolution, a teacher and a lawyer, Anastasia Pryanikova, MA, JD. We hope that you will learn a lot of useful strategies for conflict resolution in your online classroom.

Interview with Anastasia Pryanikova, MA, JD

Anastasia Pryanikova, MA, JD, is a lawyer, linguist, certified coach, and the founder of E-Studio, LLC, a coaching and training company that translates neuroscience insights into solutions in the areas of performance, collaboration, social networking, and conflict management.

From a linguist and an ESL instructor, to a corporate lawyer working internationally, to a US Small Business Administration legal adviser, Anastasia has been in the business of "changing people's minds" to facilitate high-stake conversations and decisions across borders, cultures, and industries.

As a self-proclaimed tech-geek, Anastasia also explores how technology and social media can boost influence, visibility, and strengthen human connections. You can read her blog and learn more about her work at http://brainalchemist.com.

Describe the anatomy of a conflict. How might a conflict originate online?

Conflicts are a natural part of our lives. Many people think of conflicts as something negative, but it doesn't have to be the case. We are all unique, with different life experiences, perspectives, needs, and aspirations. Even when we make decisions on our own, we often deal with competing voices in our heads. It is only natural that we won't always see eye-to-eye with others. Productive disagreements are necessary and desirable; they contain the seeds of creativity, change, and transformation. However, poorly managed conflicts may have bad consequences, including damaged relationships, uncertainty, forced changes, isolation, loss of face, tarnished reputation, and sometimes even destruction and the loss of life.

In what way are s face-to-face and online conflict similar and in what way they are different?

People are driven by the same motivating forces and goals, whether they communicate online or face-to-face. They want to be heard, understood; they want to satisfy their needs; they want to connect and have a sense of belonging to a community. The emotions are real in both face-to-face and virtual environments, and so are misunderstandings, assumptions, judgments, and power struggles that often lead to conflicts. Just because online interactions feel less personal doesn't mean they are less emotional. In fact, the opposite may be true in the cyber jungle, due to the so-called online disinhibition effect. The typical social constraints that exist when we talk face-to-face are minimal in online communication. Anonymity, invisibility, lack of visual cues and accountability often cause people to say things in cyberspace that they wouldn't say in person. The lack of direct feedback makes it easy to misunderstand and misinterpret other people's words and actions. Rushed responses online can escalate conflicts. Emotions quickly spread across online networks. The virtual world is not immune to abrasive language, bad tone, controversies, negative comments, flaming, and cyber-bullying.

When it comes to conflicts, unfortunately, our own brains can make things more difficult. Our brains have a propensity to justify our own bad behavior as a mistake, unavoidable or beyond our control. However, we are quick to assume bad intentions in others when they act badly. In addition, negative comments directly bear on our sense of fairness and social standing. The brain is sensitive to how we are treated and viewed by others. Unfortunately, the opportunities for status enhancement at somebody else's expense are easily available online. Unfair treatment triggers a stress response and can lead to negative emotional outbursts.

What are the best ways to avoid conflicts online?

- If you have an important and potentially explosive issue to discuss, opt for a face-to-face, videoconference, or phone conversation.

- Similarly, if you feel there is a potential misunderstanding or conflict brewing through online communication, pick up the phone and contact the person directly or schedule a videoconference meeting.

- When you communicate online, strive to be concise and clear. Brevity often forces us to think things through more carefully, and that extra effort is worthwhile to avoid misunderstandings.

- Don't say online what you wouldn't say to a person face-to-face. Take responsibility for what you say online. Words matter. What you do with the words matters.

- Don't post or send anything when you feel angry. You can prepare your response, but review and send it once you are calm and composed.

- Don't use abrasive language. Don't yell in ALL CAPS.

- Don't forward negative messages to others or otherwise share them publicly. Don't gossip about other people online. Don't be a bully.

- Remember that online conversations are often asynchronous. Be mindful of timing. Someone may be responding to a comment left hours earlier. When you want to respond to a specific comment in a thread, start with that person's user name to be clear who you are talking to.

- Ask yourself how your message could be interpreted by someone else.

- If you are unclear about what the other person means, ask for clarification; don't make assumptions or jump to conclusions.

- Opt for a neutral or positive intent even when you receive a somewhat negative message online. Is it possible that a person is having a bad day or dealing with some other problems that affected her communication style? Once you have your emotions under control, you can communicate more effectively.

What to do if you have gotten yourself into the online conflict no matter how much you tried to avoid it?

Pick up the phone and call the person or schedule a face-to-face or Skype meeting to clear up any misunderstandings and discuss important issues.

- Sometimes, if a conflict escalates to the point that people can't communicate effectively with each other, a neutral third party, like a mediator, can help the conflict resolution process.
- If you are a target of trolls or bullies, don't respond. Trolls and bullies use inflammatory topics or language to aggravate other people. The best strategy to deal with them is to ignore them. Don't give them any of your attention. Block or unfriend them, if possible.
- Capture and save any harassing messages as evidence and show them to someone who can help.
- Use reporting tools to remove any offensive content.
- Intervene if you see any cyber-bulling.

Do we always want to AVOID conflict in our classroom? Are there any situations when conflict is beneficial?

Building conflict competency is important for both students and adults. By practicing the skills needed to navigate conflicts effectively, in the safe environment of a classroom, students learn to question their assumptions, be better listeners, respect differences, build the common ground, explore other perspectives, reframe issues, manage their emotions, empathize, brainstorm solutions, negotiate, and collaborate. These skills can help them in their academic pursuits, future careers, and personal lives.

What can educators do to help students negotiate conflicts more effectively?

As educators, we can encourage students to become more web savvy and develop social norms and practices for respectful and responsible online communication. Here are some things educators can do:

- Engage students in discussions about their online communication styles to build self-awareness and share best practice. Case studies can also be helpful in developing conflict-competence skills.
- Model appropriate online language and behavior by moderating online forums and chat rooms.
- Educate students about online safety and security.
- Mediate conflicts among students.
- Encourage peer mediation among students.
- Pay attention to students who appear depressed or withdrawn because such symptoms can be a sign that the student is a target of cyber-bullying.

- Institute and enforce a formal policy on dealing with cyber-bullying instances.
- Compile a list of resources and phone numbers for organizations that deal with online identity theft, cyber-bullying, etc.

As we can see, there are many strategies that you can implement in your classroom to provide a peaceful and welcoming atmosphere and to diminish negative interactions —so that you and your students or trainees can enjoy yourselves. Just remember that it is almost impossible to avoid misunderstandings online. Don't judge yourself too harshly if you have found yourself in such a situation. Using Anastasia's advice, remember that "interpersonal conflicts are not something to be afraid of or to be avoided at any cost. Instead, we need to learn how to navigate them effectively and grow from the experience. And remember that while hot buttons are always present, reactions are optional."

Tool 2: Plagiarism and Cheating Prevention

Another tool that will make your online interactions pleasant and will increase your enjoyment of the online environment is maintaining academic integrity and implementing a plagiarism prevention technique. According to the Merriam-Webster Online Dictionary, to plagiarize means

- to steal and pass off (the ideas or words of another) as one's own;
- to use (another's production) without crediting the source;
- to commit literary theft;
- to present as new and original an idea or product derived from an existing source.

In other words, plagiarism and cheating are an act of fraud involving purposeful or unaware stealing, and lying about this stealing. Therefore, it is crucial for the teacher to prevent plagiarism in his classroom. Unfortunately, it is much easier to plagiarize online and much harder to detect such actions. Research shows that around 75 percent of students have engaged in some form of plagiarism online. So what are the ways to prevent this situation? Here are some strategies that will show online teachers and trainers how to avoid plagiarism online.

1. Provide a definition of plagiarism to your students and give concrete examples.

   Often students do not know what plagiarism is. It is impossible to avoid something you do not understand. One way to provide relevant information is to organize small group activities that result in students' discussing contemporary examples of plagiarism. Providing students with examples and identifying the reasons for avoiding plagiarism and repercussions for such actions will also help establish the baseline in your classroom and will more likely diminish instances of plagiarism. Showing students how obvious plagiarism often is because of the evident change in writing style that comes with pasting in another person's work can serve to discourage the practice. Facilitation of small- and large-group discussions, where students define plagiarism in their own words, and/or their own language, can lead to intercultural insights and serve as a useful preventative strategy

   Note: You need to understand that definitions of plagiarism as well as attitudes towards plagiarism are predicated on culturally based assumptions. What is considered a taboo in one culture might be perfectly acceptable in another. If you deal with people from different backgrounds, make sure to emphasize the importance of avoiding plagiarism in your particular country and educational setting.

2. Provide students with opportunities to learn and practice how to cite and paraphrase.

   Citing others and giving credits to other's work is a learned skill, and you cannot expect students to avoid plagiarism without providing them first with the tools that teach them proper citation.

3. Set time limits for student activities, including tests and other high-stakes assignments. When students know that they have a shorter period of time to complete an assignment or a quiz, they will more likely avoid cheating and searching for someone else's work, but will use what they know to answer the questions.

4. Assign various types of work frequently in a semester to establish a track record and have various bases for assessments.

   It is good practice to measure your students' work with various types of assessments. The greater the variety of assessments you have, the fewer opportunities there are for plagiarism. In addition, having students' records collected from these activities is useful because they can help you compare their writing samples and see any deviation from the norm. Project work that includes showing the final piece of work to other students before or after marking adds the pressure of peer review, which can increase the quality of work and discourage plagiarism.

5. Test randomization

   Most learning management systems allow you to randomize your tests, so different students will have different orders of items on their quizzes. This way it will be harder for them to plagiarize each other's work.

6. Strategic grade weight assignments

   Make assessments that are hard to control, such as online quizzes, just a small part of the final grade, giving more weight to other forms of assessment that measure deeper knowledge and demand higher thinking processes.

7. Use synchronous classes to assess your students' knowledge.

   If you incorporate synchronous interactions, try to conduct main assessments during your virtual class.

8. Use technology to check for plagiarism.

   Some programs such as Turn-It-In show you how to check for plagiarism online. You just need to insert a sample writing of your student into the program and you will receive a detailed report on it.

9. Create written contracts.

   Contract creation is one of the most powerful tools for changing a behavior. Somehow, when we put things into written words, they become "legal," "serious," and "for real." Contracts provide us with the feeling of commitment and accountability. It is much harder to break a written contract than a verbal one.

Note: We hope that all strategies above will help you prevent plagiarism and cheating in your classroom. However, cheating and plagiarism are not only the responsibility of the student. Online teachers must maintain open communication with the students, provide timely feedback, and incorporate all the strategies for connection and engagement that we have described above.

How to check for plagiarism

There are several signs of cheating and plagiarism that you can look for in your students' work:

- Mixed formatting of citations: Often students who plagiarize use different citation systems (e.g., MLA vs. APA) interchangeably.
- Mixed formatting of the text: Often when students copy information from other sites they forget to delete the URL address or some other marks of the web-based text left on the paper. Their papers might also have some strange formatting that results from cutting and pasting from the web into a Word doc.
- Assignment completion: When you receive students' work, ask yourself: "Are all parts of the assignment covered?" Sometimes you can see an elaborate answer to one question and almost nothing for another; this could be a sign of plagiarism.
- Mixed writing style: If you notice that the written style of your student changes markedly throughout the paper, it might be a sign of plagiarism or cheating. Also, compare the style of your students' work with a writing sample from your records.

Secret #3: Managing Your Mind

As teachers we live to give. In fact, we give so much that we often feel awkward or even guilty when we are placed in a position of receiving. The thought of taking time for ourselves and meeting our personal needs is almost a taboo for many of us. Therefore, many teachers are overworked and overstressed. The worst burden falls especially on those who spend a lot of time with technology. We get "absorbed" by our computers and the Internet, and it almost runs our lives. In reality, ever since the Internet became a part of our reality, our attention has shrunk, our workload has increased, and our overall well-being has been compromised.

Do you check your e-mail several times a day? How about every hour? Do you feel the urge to check several sites at a time while you are working online? Do you take work- related phone calls even when you're out with your family? Do you need to stay online even when you're on vacation? Do you feel lost if there is no Internet connection? How about when you have left your cell phone at home?

We live in a state of hypermind, where we constantly switch from one topic to another without resting in between. We work with frequent interruptions and consider it to be a normal part of our lives. One minute we are engaged with an important project and the next minute someone sends us an e-mail or texts us with an urgent matter that needs attention. This constant moving back and forth interrupts our focus and creates frustration, making it difficult for us to concentrate. We become almost addicted to technology and feel the need to be constantly using it. However, in reality, we should learn how to use technology, not to be used by it. Our "smart phones" do not force us to answer the call. The 24/7 Internet connection does not push us to search for everything there is, and just because e-mail can be sent and received instantly, you don't have to reply to it right away. Taking back control of your life and your mind is critical in order to live a happy and joyful existence as an online teacher.

We were not born with a computer in our hand, and being attached to it is not our natural form of being. Because we try to make our connection to technology an organic process, stress (and often depression) becomes an inevitable presence in our hypermind. Stress occurs when we leave the present moment and mentally go to either the past or the future: "I can't believe this student wrote me this e-mail"; "I have so many papers yet to correct today." Such thoughts are not addressing the present moment but are pointing at the moment before or after the one that is right now. At times like this we feel that we have failed at something and at the same time have not gotten enough done, and we dread starting to do things that we need to accomplish. Our minds keep telling us the same thing over and over, such as "I wish I had more time," "I could have done more if I…" We have 65,000 thoughts per day, the same thoughts over and over. It is not surprising that our online teaching experience becomes so dull and so stressful. Yet again, we are here to remind you that teaching online can be highly enjoyable — for reasons of both professional reward and lifestyle freedom. It also allows you to live the life of your dreams, remember? Stress and hypermind are probably not a part of your perfect picture, so let's talk about what you can do to avoid these experiences.

How do we handle our stress and calm our hyperminds? First of all, we need to remember that nothing is really worth getting stressed out over. Somehow in the end it always works out. Stress is poisonous to our body, our psyche, and our productivity. It keeps us in a constant state of fear and disables us. When you catch yourself stressing over the amount of work you need to do...stop! Look at your ideal schedule that we discussed before. Shift to being productive — just keep going through the list of things you identified for yourself that day. Having a time limit will remind you that your work will eventually be over; let your brain focus on the most important activity, then the next, one at a time.

It is also important to engage in daily habits that help you stay centered and eliminate stress before it even happens. Make sure to add nonnegotiable "you" time to your "ideal schedule." The best way to do it is to have some time for yourself in the morning right after you wake up and start your day by making yourself strong. For each of us the process is different, but one thing needs to happen: we need to reach a state of stillness of the mind, a state of clarity and focus. This state cannot be achieved if the first thing you do is open your computer and start searching the net or checking your e-mails. Actually, no technology should be used during the process of making yourself strong. Instead, you should use time to connect with yourself through either yoga, meditation, exercise, walking, or just sitting still for at least twenty minutes. We already hear some of you saying, "But I don't have twenty minutes to spare in my day, especially in the morning. To which we will reply by paraphrasing the wisdom of the yogis: If you don't have twenty minutes for yourself, you will probably need two hours! Being still does not mean you stop being productive. It means that you bring your mind to a natural state of calmness from which you start your day. Believe us, if you begin practicing giving to yourself as the first thing in your day, you will react to people and circumstances better, you will be more productive, and even more positive situations will seem to come to your life. The quality of your experience will dramatically improve.

Giving to yourself should not end in the morning. It needs to continue throughout the day. In your ideal schedule set some time aside between the main blocks for work and use this time to get away from your computer. Go for a ten-to 15-minute walk around a block, stretch, play with your kid or a pet. Do whatever you can to unglue yourself from your desk and from your computer. The trick here is to avoid getting "fixed" by another technological gadget. Turning on the TV or using your cell will still contribute to your hypermind, and will not create the focus and calmness that you really need when you work long hours online. Besides, don't forget about the importance of eating well, sleeping enough, hydrating, and exercising.

All of these self-giving techniques are incredibly important for building your well-being and enjoying your life as well as your work online. We already hear some of you saying, "But these activities take too much of my time. I can't spend so much time on me!" If you use these strategies you will actually be more productive and a better giver. Also, if you incorporate them into your ideal schedule you will see how natural living this new lifestyle will become and how much more joy it will bring to you and to others. Taking care of oneself is a number-one priority for any person, especially for those who "give" for a living, such as teachers. We all need to start with our "being," which extends beyond "knowing" and "doing," that we addressed in the previous chapters and constitutes the core of the Golden Climate, which we will discuss in detail in the next chapter.

CHAPTER 3

HOW TO BE IS THE KEY

"I've learned that people will forget what you said, people will forget what you did, but people will never forget how you made them feel."

-Maya Angelou (American Poet, b.1928)

The Importance of Being

In the previous sections we discussed that both knowing and doing are important for effective teaching online. However, there is a third dimension, which we have mentioned at times, and which lies at the core of the Golden Climate: the dimension of being. How to be with your students and trainees, so that they will engage, perform well, and develop a capacity for autonomy — be successful in their learning — is the subject of this chapter. What you know is important: knowing about your own fears concerning online teaching, for example, and how these might be overcome; knowing your subject matter, so that you can enrich your students' learning experience as a resource and a guide; knowing that adapting students' work to their needs and experience — making course requirements negotiable where possible — will lead to more successful outcomes. What you do is also important: knowledge needs to be put into practice if the course is to be fruitful for the learners and the teacher, and we have mentioned several ways to improve how you communicate with your learners online. There is, however, an element missing. In the virtual classroom, we find that "best practice" has its limits: it is not best for everyone, because every student is different, and every student-teacher relationship is different. Best practice is like telling everyone to wear the same clothes because a fashion expert told you that those clothes are good for students. Best practice is not always your best option, and can seem like a rigid, one-size-fits-all approach. What is the alternative? To let your students come alive as individuals, who have enrolled in your course because they want to learn and grow according to their interests and needs — and to foster their expression of this energy in the learning experience. The Golden Climate is about giving them the opportunity to dialogue with you on every aspect of their learning, and through this process to define with you a learning experience adapted to their needs, experience, and interests. To do this, you need to be with your students in a certain way. Rather than dictating to a student what she must do, you need to create a "space" in which the student can try things, learn, have fun, and grow, in which the learning experience is negotiated and fostered, and in which the student feels safe in initiating work to do and in taking the risk to explore new ideas. Through the creation of this interrelational space — through their relationship with you — a student can reach her potential in your course. Success in distance learning depends less on what you know and what you do than on your being with your students in a certain way. If students don't feel that they can bloom in their relationship with you, they will turn away from both you and their learning. The excitement of learning comes from the possibilities of growth that the learning experience promises; this chapter is about how to make this happen.

The quality of the relationship that you create with your students will define the quality of your presence in their learning experience during the course. If your presence has been facilitative to a student's growth, they will carry your presence with them as an inner strength in future learning experiences. You need to know that despite the distance and the technological interface, you can connect with your students in a powerful way that can help them to become strong and independent learners, the kind of learner that we all need to be in order to enjoy success in any facet of modern life. The important thing is to make room in your interrelational space for your students to be, to bring you their needs, experience, and interests, where they can trust that you will listen to them, build on what they say, inspire them, and help them to create a learning experience with which they want to engage. It is when your students respond positively to your trust, respect, listening, suggesting, providing vision, discussing possibilities, flexibility to accommodate their needs, empathic reaching out, curiosity —w hen both the student and you are feeling vibrant, creative, and productive in your interrelational space — that is when The Golden Climate can come about.

You need to believe that your relationship with your students is the number-one key to success — theirs and yours. Your students will sense if you are just going through the motions, pushing buttons and posting content, without reaching out to them in a humble, respectful, and enthusiastic way, with the core message being "here's a space where we can go on a journey together, grow together, and have a fascinating experience along the way — and enjoy ourselves. I'll be here as a resource, facilitator, guide, and negotiator, to help you initiate and develop a piece of work that is relevant to your needs, within the social context of the virtual classroom. I am concerned about your educational well-being in this course." This message needs to come from the heart. Imagine a dancer who memorizes her routine. She is aware of her fears and limitations and she develops a choreography that emphasizes her strengths. She spends hours and hours rehearsing the moves and, finally, she performs each move with perfection. However, if her being is separate from her doing, she will never capture our attention as much as another dancer who puts her heart into her dance and becomes the dance itself. Like this dancer, an online teacher must not only move through the motions, but go beyond them to communicate the core message as stated above to her audience. To do so in the online context you might need to challenge your beliefs and change the way you see yourself as a teacher. You must realize that distance learning is as much about building strong emotional bonds with your students as it is about building knowledge. When you build relationships online you build an environment of trust and care that allows students to take control of their academic growth and be autonomous yet not alone in their journey. For these relationships to be successful, it is not only what you do that counts: it is how you be with others that matters.

The Golden Climate therefore is not a substance that can be measured by the amount of messages you post online, or by your time log. When you build relationships with others that support growth and autonomy while creating a sense of connection, i.e., when you build the Golden Climate, you must also be receptive to the intentions and dispositions of other people and negotiate your interactions based on these dynamics. Willing yourself to be a great teacher online will not get you to your goal. If you want to create a welcoming classroom, you must BE welcoming, not just apply welcoming strategies. If you want your students to feel comfortable sharing their ideas and thoughts online, you must BE the person who is comfortable with such sharing. If you want your students to enjoy your class, you must BE enjoying it too. Therefore, your role online changes from the giver of knowledge or "doing" to providing emotional support, building connections, and feeling the dynamics of the classroom: i.e., your role shifts to the realm of being. Certainly, if you have been teaching in a traditional way, where your role is to be authoritarian and detached and to transmit knowledge, this new way of seeing yourself requires a paradigm shift — a process that is not easily implemented and that takes time. The successful engagement, autonomy, enjoyment, and performance of your students depends on your making this shift.

The foundation for the Golden Climate (figure 1) is the teacher-learner relationship. This means that The Golden Climate in Distance Learning is not just constructed by the teacher, but by both the teacher and the learner together. With each learner, the teacher will construct a relationship within which the learner will succeed, or fail. The teacher brings her capacity to be with the other, to be concerned for the other's needs, to foster the growth of the other, to be humble and learn from the other; her professional knowledge of what to do and the assumptions that underpin this knowledge; and her personal knowledge about how she feels about the online teaching and learning context and, if she has doubts and fears, how these might be overcome. The learner brings his capacity to be with the other, his willingness to learn, an awareness of certain of his needs, and doubts and fears about whether he will like the teacher and be able to learn with her in a way that will excite his imagination and curiosity and make him feel alive, inspired, and that he is growing and discovering his potential in the learning process and producing his best work.

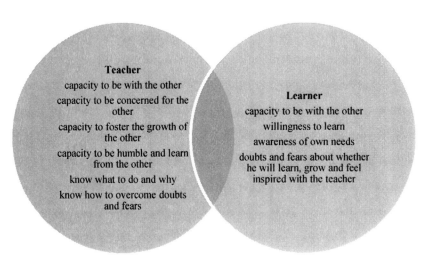

Figure 1. The Foundation of the Golden Climate

In the intersection, where the two beings interrelate, is the space where the Golden Climate is constructed, where the groundwork is laid for engagement and learning. It is a space where the teacher and learner can go on a journey together, grow together, and have a fascinating experience along the way. The Golden Climate that you create with the learner online will help her to succeed even in times of struggle — to dare to take risks and struggle — because at the very core of this climate lies emotional support from the teacher.

The Role of Emotions in the Golden Climate

Since affective aspects are less noticeable in distance learning than in a face-to-face classroom (Meyer & Turner, 2006), not too much attention has been devoted to the importance of emotion online. Historically, emotions have also been seen as existing separately from cognition, and are therefore often discarded as something that should not be trusted (Damasio, 1999). For several centuries, emotions have been seen as not crucial for cognition and thinking, and even inferior to thinking (Damasio, 1999). Even in ancient Greece, Plato divided the mind into separate and conflicting parts: reason, desire, and emotion. The latter two parts made it difficult for the mind to be clear. Later on, Descartes's famous philosophy, "Cogito ergo sum," equated thought with existence and excluded emotional aspects from being. It was not until the twentieth century that emotions began to be seen as crucial for thinking and learning. In psychology, James came up with a classification of emotions, and Gardner developed a system of multiple intelligences. Despite the fact that in a traditional education, affective factors have finally gained their proper place, in distance education there is still not enough research that investigates the effect of emotions on learning at a distance. The limited research that exists in distance learning on the subject of emotions demonstrates that they are important contributors to student motivation (Dirkx & Smith, 2009), student satisfaction, learner connection (Kostina, 2011), and successful learning online (La Ganza, 2001, 2004). Our research shows that distance learning is an extremely emotional experience for both teachers and students. Further, the dispositions and feelings of the people on the "other side of cyberspace" are particularly transparent.

The role of emotion thus becomes vital in the online environment: we cannot stress enough the importance of the emotional support that the online teacher provides to her students. This emotional support will lay the foundation for the Golden Climate that we will discuss in the following section.

The Golden Climate in Distance Learning

The Golden Climate in Distance Learning can be understood in terms of the theory of the Dynamic Interrelational Space (DIS) proposed by LaGanza (2004) and supported by Kostina (2011). The DIS is relevant to online learning, a context that requires learners to work on an autonomous basis, as it explains how learner autonomy might be encouraged and maintained in the teaching-learning context. Understanding the DIS will enable you to create with your learners the optimal climate — The Golden Climate — in which to apply the pedagogy that we have discussed above to its greatest effect, and thus to optimize engagement, enjoyment, performance, and autonomy. In this climate, the learner is working on an autonomous basis on work he has initiated independently or with others, which is relevant to his needs and interests. The learner is working creatively and productively, involving the constructive criticism of others in the process, and has negotiated with the teacher a learning experience adapted to the learner's needs and interests. The learner is supported by the teacher, who is a resource, guide, facilitator, and negotiator, but who is holding back from influencing the learner's work and learning experience as the learner develops his piece of work.

The key to the Golden Climate is teacher-learner interrelation, not just interaction. According to the Macquarie Dictionary (1981), the noun "interrelation" implies a "reciprocal relation"; a "relation" is "a particular way of being associated, connected, allied": "the mode or kind of connection between one person and another." Significantly, human beings can relate to one another verbally or nonverbally. The verb "relate" means "to bring into or establish association, connection, or relation," and also implies action. "Interaction" is not a synonym for "interrelation." While interaction involves "reciprocal action" between persons, it does not imply "establishing association, connection, or relation": other forms of affective engagement.

Another concept that is connected with interrelation is autonomy. If the online classroom context actively encourages knowledge generation through social interaction, and thus interrelating, between the teacher and the learner, and among learners, it might also be a context in which learners have influence over the learning process and the work to be done. In this kind of context, learners are necessarily engaged in developing their capacity to be autonomous.

The DIS theory proposes that it is the notion of interrelating — verbal and nonverbal — and its implied affective engagement that will allow a new understanding of what is at stake in encouraging the development of a learner's capacity for autonomy. Any factors limiting the development of learner autonomy online must necessarily be related to the participants in that context. To the individual learner faced with initiating and developing his own piece of work in his way, engaging actively and meaningfully in the learning experience in distance learning could be a daunting, perhaps even prohibitive, prospect — even to a learner who feels independent in other contexts. Within all humans, there is a dread of isolation. According to the psychoanalyst Winnicott (1965), the fear of loss of communication with others is an acute human fear; loss of communication for an infant can be "shattering" (p. 183). Lashbrook (2000), in a study of college students aged nineteen to twenty-three found that the "fear of isolation" not only motivated young adults to adhere to and conform within peer groups, but also motivated them "empathetically" to draw others in to their social groupings (p. 752). These bonds, Lashbrook says, "constitute a fundamental 'glue' for society" (p. 750). In this way, it seems, the fear of isolation informs our grouping into families and communities, and our anxiety about the dissolution of the same. Should the family, social group, or community be seen to provide a "good-enough" (Winnicott, 1965, p. 145) nurturing or "holding" (Winnicott 1971, p. 131) environment for its members as they grow, they might reach a high level of maturity and independence. They may even choose to leave the group to become part of another. As an apparent reflection of this group-based maturational process, the education of individuals in our society is mostly arranged in groups set up by community-based institutions to allow individuals to mature through particular learning experiences, including peer and teacher relationships, and which individuals will eventually leave.

In the distance learning context, what are the implications for social cohesion and identity when the teacher refrains from subjecting learners to her influence; when each learner is initiating and developing his own piece of work in his own way; when both the subject and the developmental process of each learner's work is different from each other's and surpasses the limits of the teacher's knowledge? The answer would appear to lie in achieving and maintaining a climate of social connectedness among classroom participants. Through drawing upon his classroom relationships, the learner faced with initiating and directing a piece of work could overcome the fears associated with working "alone" enough to take the necessary risks concerning creativity and originality, a condition in which "the individual is able to come to grips with himself, to develop the courage to give up his defenses and face his true self" (Tenenbaum, 1961, p. 305). What might be involved, however, in the paradoxical challenge of achieving social connectedness while developing learner autonomy online? An understanding of the psychosocial dynamics involved in this process could be expected to help both the teacher and the learner in realizing this achievement.

Breen and Mann (1997) have highlighted from a social perspective the "dynamic" nature of the "teaching-learning process" (p. 144). These authors believe that the "dynamics of the social relationships in the classroom…constantly impact upon the learner's opportunities to be autonomous," and that understanding how this may occur "seems to be an essential element in a pedagogy for autonomy" (p. 145). The dynamics involved operate within learners who "shift" between "phase[s]" (p. 143) related to dependence and independence, and within teachers and the classroom group who shift between phases related to autocracy and collaboration; however, the dynamics do not operate between the learners and the teachers/group (p. 143). The phases are not constructed between teachers and learners. These writers perceive the social world as "impacting" upon learners; but what of the essential elements of this social context: the participants themselves? How might learners and teachers be constructing their social world?

Figure 2, the DIS model, represents a range of interrelational climates in distance learning. The central issue is that of learner autonomy: in order to create The Golden Climate in Distance Learning, the teacher needs to hold back enough to foster a learner's becoming an independent producer of work relevant to their own needs and experience — the optimal conditions for engagement, autonomy, enjoyment, and performance. There are forces in the teacher and learner that act against the learner's independence:

the teacher's instinct says, "Keep control!" The learner's instinct says, "Ask the teacher!" There is a continual tension in the teacher-learner relationship, between the teacher's trying to influence, or not to influence, the learner's work and learning experience, and the learner's trying to seek, or not trying to seek, the teacher's influence. Each quadrant in figure 2 represents a different phase of teacher/learner tension, or "interrelational climate," as well as phases of tension within teachers and within learners. It is not sufficient to define learner autonomy as a learner's taking control of or taking responsibility for his learning. Learner autonomy is an achievement, attained interrelationally between the teacher and learner. The extent to which a learner can grow toward being able to work on an autonomous basis depends on whether the teacher and learner, together, can create a climate conducive to the learner's autonomy. The interrelational climate most conducive to the learner's autonomy is Q3 in figure 2 below; this is the Golden Climate.

The core features of the DIS are the dualities, or sources of inner tension (T+/T- and L+/L-) that characterize the teacher-learner relationship. These sources of tension influence to what extent the interrelational climate created between the teacher and the learner might be conducive to the learner's autonomy. T+ signifies that the teacher is trying to influence the learning experience; T- denotes that the teacher is resisting this influence. L+ indicates the learner is willing to accept the teacher's influence; and L- signifies the learner is resisting the teacher's influence and/or his desire to seek empowerment to influence the learning experience in some way. The teacher-learner interrelational climate changes constantly during the learning process, as the teacher influences the learner or holds back, and as the learner seeks the teacher's influence or works on a more autonomous basis. The quadrants show four possible climates in a teaching-learning context. In quadrant 1, the teacher seeks to influence the learning experience and/or to assist the learner, while the learner accepts the teacher's influence or seeks the teacher's assistance. In quadrant 2, the teacher resists influencing the learner, as he/she encourages the learner to initiate and define his work and learning experience. The learner here seeks the teacher's assistance concerning work to be done or some clarification of the learning experience.

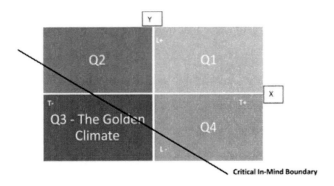

X: teacher seeks influence T +/ resists influence T-/ Y: student seeks influence L +/ rejects influence L-

Q 1	T+ Teacher seeks to influence the learning experience and/or to assist the learner. L + Learner accepts Teacher's influence on the learning experience and the assistance offered, or seeks Teachers' assistance
Q 2	T- Teacher resistant: encourages Learner to initiate and/or define his or her work and/or define the learning experience L + Learner seeks Teacher's assistance concerning work to be done or some clarification of the learning experience
Q 3	T+ Teacher seeks to influence the learning experience and/or to assist the learner. L - Learner seeks empowerment: indicates to Teacher that he or she would like to struggle alone to initiate and/or define his or her own work and/or define the learning experience
Q 4	T- Teacher resistant: encourages/ allows Learner to initiate and/or define his or her work and/or define the learning experience L- Learner seeks empowerment: indicates to Teacher that he or she would like to struggle alone to initiate and/or define his or her own work and/ or define the learning experience

Figure 2. The Dynamic Interrelational Space model of teacher-learner interrelating in terms of learner autonomy, showing *The Golden Climate in Distance Learning* in Q3

In quadrant 3, the teacher resists influencing the learner as she encourages or allows the learner to define his work and to define his learning experience. The learner here seeks to remain empowered and struggles to initiate and define his learning experience. In this quadrant, the learner is the most independent, potentially enjoying a vibrant, creative, and productive learning experience that he has adapted to his needs and interests in negotiation with the teacher, and in which he is supported by the constructive criticism of his colleagues and feels that he is doing his best possible work. The teacher is supporting his investigation through her role of resource, guide, facilitator, and negotiator, and as we will discuss below, communicates to the learner that she has the learner "in mind." This is The Golden Climate in Distance Learning to which we as teachers need to aspire. In quadrant 4, the teacher seeks to influence the learning experience or to assist the learner in some way. The learner seeks empowerment and indicates to the teacher that he would like to continue to struggle alone in order to initiate and define his own work and learning experience.

As mentioned above, the development of a learner's capacity to be autonomous mainly occurs in the Golden Q3 interrelational climate. Let's look in more detail at what this climate implies for the teacher and the learner, for even though it is a climate that promises great potential reward, maintaining it involves developing particular teacher and learner qualities to overcome challenging emotions. Indeed, a Q3 climate is characterized by restraint and some discomfort on the part of the teacher. The learner here struggles in his learning process. The learner makes mistakes, experiences doubt and uncertainty, and resists appealing to the teacher for appropriate answers and solutions. Besides developing a capacity for resisting the influence of the teacher, the learner must also develop a capacity for persistence in using outside resources, as well as the teacher, for learning. The teacher, on the other hand, must develop a capacity for communicating to the learner and express to the learner that she is concerned for the student's well-being in this educational process: that she has the learner "in mind." The teacher also needs to be able to cope with her own anxieties associated with facilitating the learning process, such as worry about whether or not to offer help to the learner should the learner not seek the teachers' influence, and if so, how. This climate shows that a learner's capacity for development of autonomy can vary with different teachers depending on their interrelation. Therefore, learner autonomy is only meaningful in the psychosocial context and only when the teacher and the learner interrelate. Hence, we propose that the term learner autonomy is problematic because it only emphasizes one side of the dynamic relationship whereby the learner self-governs in isolation from external factors. The paradox of learner autonomy is that the learner can be autonomous while in facilitating relationship with the teacher who is present externally, or, after satisfactory experiences of autonomy, internally. Therefore, learner autonomy is the capacity of a learner to sustain a predominantly third quadrant interrelational climate in his or her experience — or a Q3 capacity.

Interrelational climates are not static phenomena. Rather, the modes of teaching and learning continually change the interrelational climate, which shifts among all four quadrants in the course of each lesson observed. The changing modes of teaching give rise to continual climate shifts between quadrants, though a particular interrelational climate would usually prevail in one or two quadrants during certain phases of a course. In the introductory lesson phase, for example, the interrelational climate can be mainly in Q1, whereas during the presentation development and performance stage the climate is often in Q3, with the learners empowered in producing their presentations, delivering them, and leading subsequent discussion and criticism with the rest of the group. In the course of each lesson, however, all climates are repeatedly experienced, often in more subtle ways than in the obvious examples cited above.

Figure 2 shows a line going through quadrants 2 and 3 to quadrant 4. This line is the Critical In-Mind Boundary (CIB), which demonstrates the place where teacher-learner interrelating risks breaking down because of a lack of rigor. The CIB is a feature predominately of Q3 because in the other three interrelational climates either the teacher or the learner (or both) are seeking interrelation over the content, the structure, or other features of the learning experience. In the Golden Q3 climate, both the teacher and the learner are resistant to interacting at the academic level. This situation may be difficult to maintain in a distance classroom wherein the teacher and the learner are physically far from each other. If the CIB is crossed, the online learner might feel isolated, while the teacher might also feel unsuccessful in fostering learner autonomy. The exact position of the CIB depends on each teacher-learner relationship. Usually, the teacher receives a sign from the student that the CIB is about to be crossed, and that their connection is breaking down. The teacher might feel a loss of touch, after which the learner might drop out without a word.

Crossing the Critical In-Mind Boundary

In the case of teaching in a Q3 interrelational climate, encouraging the development of a learner's capacity to be autonomous, failure to maintain interrelating by communicating to the learner that you have their well-being and that of their project in mind (see the three domains of concern below) can lead to a weakening of the teacher-learner relationship. When this relationship is weak, the risk is that the learner's experience of isolation and fear of failure might affect the quality of the educative experience to the extent that the learner feels that continuing his work in the course is futile. At this point, teacher-learner interrelating has crossed the CIB. It can be assumed that the position of the CIB would be different for each teacher-learner relationship and would thus be relevant primarily on an individual level. In each case, the level of teacher recognition when approaching the CIB with a learner could be expected to be either overt, covert, or lacking.

- *Overt recognition*

Prior to crossing the CIB with an individual learner, the teacher might receive strong indications from the learner that the relationship was breaking down. These might include

- the learner's seeking confirmation by e-mail or phone that the teacher still has the learner "in-mind": that the three domains of in-mind concern (discourses) discussed below remain part of teacher-learner interrelating;
- an attempt on the part of the learner to change the Interrelational Climate to, for example, Q2, as the learner tries actively to engage the teacher in regard to the work at hand.

- *Covert recognition*

The teacher might recognize a "loss of touch" feeling in regard to one learner or the learners generally, and make an effort to improve the quality of interrelating through demonstrations of concern for the learner(s) via the three in-mind discourses discussed below.

- *Lack of recognition*

It cannot be assumed that a teacher would be aware of the status of her relationship with each learner in a class, particularly in a relatively large classroom group. While believing that she was maintaining a good enough quality of relating in a Golden Q3 climate to assure the educative quality of the learning experience, the less sensitive or overwhelmed teacher might unwittingly "lose touch" with some learners. Further, it cannot be assumed that the learner would give any indication that the Critical In-mind Boundary was being approached. The learner might drop out without a word as a reaction to the threatened or actual breakdown of the relationship and its protection from isolation and the failure of the work at hand.

Thus, the relationship between the teacher and learner is effective within the CIB and breaks down beyond it. The role of emotions here is vital; in order for the teacher to successfully foster the learner's autonomy, she must engage intellectually and emotionally with the learner. This emotional investment will also allow the teacher to feel connected to the student while they are engaged in initiating and developing their piece of work. In-mind student-teacher dialogue can be evidenced through various communicative exchanges, whereby the teacher shows her concern and the student acknowledges it. In-mind interaction can also be nonverbal, even online. In the face-to-face classroom, the blink of a learner's eye can appear to signal a refusal of what a teacher was offering. In the online environment, student-teacher interaction can be interrupted by the student's sudden silence or ongoing lack of responsiveness. Nevertheless, the teacher-learner relationship must be maintained. In the following section we will provide you with the secret to becoming a master of the Golden Climate.

How to "Be" a Master of the Golden Climate

As we have mentioned throughout this book, the role of the teacher online is different from that of a traditional teacher. In order to become a master of the Golden Climate, the teacher must be a certain way in order to hold or support the student emotionally and intellectually as he is developing his capacity to work on an autonomous basis in Q3: to encourage the development of learner autonomy without pushing the student towards isolation. Should a teacher wish to teach in the Golden Q3 interrelational climate, where learning is a result of learners' producing knowledge meaningful to themselves rather than being consumers of the knowledge constructions of others, then the learner might not have received more than the barest guidelines concerning his possible directions in the course. Much might depend upon the learner's capacity to overcome his fear of working "alone" in a relatively unstructured context and engage meaningfully in his learning experience, including with other participants in the learning context. What might save the learner from foundering is the mode of teacher-learner interrelating. Most importantly, the teacher needs to communicate her concern for the learners' well-being in his educational experience. The teacher's engagement needs to be emotional, intellectual, and sustained over time. When the teacher's concern is communicated to learners, it is perceived by them and carried with them as the teacher's presence. If, on the contrary, the teacher is not successful in communicating concern in the online context, there is a risk of crossing the CIB. Instead of engagement, enjoyment, performance, and autonomy, the student and the teacher will feel isolated and unsuccessful. There are three secrets that the teacher must learn in order to create and maintain The Golden Climate in Distance Learning. The teacher must be a perceptive resource, a participant observer, and a supporter of each learner's individuality. These three domains of concern may be described as follows:

Secret 1: Be a Perceptive Resource

"I'm here as a 'perceptive' resource with your work in mind."

As a *perceptive resource*, the teacher needs to respond to the student's inquiries and requests with a quick apprehension and understanding of what might help the learner to find meaning in the learning process. This could include the teacher's

- inviting consultation with learners and welcoming it when it occurs;
- replying to a learner's requests in ways that indicate the learner's questions have some priority in the teacher's schedule and that the teacher is concerned to provide help that is meaningful for that particular learner;
- following up on situations where there is or has been uncertainty.

Secret 2: Be a Participant Observer

"I'm here as a participant-observer in the learning process and I'm keeping in mind what is meaningful for you in your development as a learner."

As a *participant-observer*, the teacher indicates that she has the learner's meaningful development in-mind. This could include the teacher's

- using individual learning contracts and negotiated topics for pieces of work;
- indicating in dialogue with the learner a genuine interest in what the learner might discover;
- indicating in dialogue with the learner empathy for what the learner is thinking and feeling in the learning experience;
- making an occasional discreet inquiry, for example, "Have you thought about this?" perhaps leading to the learner's responding/feeling surprised and reassured: "Heavens! She's thinking about me!"

Secret 3: Be Supportive of Each Learner's Individuality

"I'm keeping in mind the experiences that might have informed your learning focus; I'm trying to ensure your individuality can be voiced through your learning experience."

In being supportive of each learner's individuality, the teacher ensures that individuality can be voiced through the learning experience. This could include the teacher's

- encouraging discussion at times on non — work-related matters;

- seeking the learner's opinions about areas of the learner's expertise/experience;
- reminding the learner of a previous comment or idea of the learner's that might connect with and enrich the learner's new suggestion or initiative.

Conclusion:
Redefining the Teacher's Presence and Teacher's Role Online

Self-directed learning on an autonomous basis does not have to be an alienating experience for either the teacher or the learner. An important and legitimate role of the online teacher seeking to create a Golden Q3 inter-relational climate is to maintain the human quality of the interrelational dynamics by letting the learner know that the teacher not only has that person in-mind but also recognizes the importance to that person of feeling "held" by the teaching context, including constructing a firm identity as part of the classroom group. When the teacher communicates to the learner that she has the learner in-mind, the teaching-learning relationship is being maintained. Having a learner in-mind defines the "presence" of the teacher in the teaching/ learning context. When the teacher is not present in this way, the learning experience is in danger of losing its educative quality, and the learner is in danger of dropping out, not feeling "held" enough to grow in the teaching/ learning context that has been created. According to this definition of a teacher's presence, it is conceivable that a teacher in a face-to-face situation in a classroom might not be "present" for some learners, whereas an online teacher encouraging learner autonomy, conscious of demonstrating to her learners that she has them in-mind, could, while not physically present, be firmly present in their minds and creating a context conducive to an enriching learning experience.

CHAPTER 4

AN APPETITE FOR MORE…

In this chapter we have compiled some frequently asked questions and answers that might help you in your journey through teaching and training online. We invite you to continue this conversation in our online forum www.thegoldenclimateindistancelearning.com

Why are there such conflicting data on the effectiveness of distance learning? Some studies show that it is a very effective environment while others demonstrate that many students fail online.

Distance learning cannot be used as a one-size-fits-all environment. Unfortunately, many distance learning programs are still structured within the modernist approach, which emphasizes standardization and creation of a unified curriculum for all. This is a formula for an impoverished learning experience and high learner dropout rates. The distance learning field needs to recognize the need for postmodern thinking, which focuses on each individual's needs and acknowledges that to know something about the world the learner needs to investigate various perspectives and socially validate his conclusions. Online educators and pedagogical designers need to make available a flexible learning space and accompany learners on their journey as they initiate, investigate, and discuss the progress of their pieces of work. All the while, the teacher needs to be aware of how she might "hold" each learner within the teacher-learner relationship, so as to provide a secure climate in which the learner can take risks in his learning experience as he moves toward independence creatively, fulfilling his needs and pursuing his interests, with a hand in his destiny, and bloom.

Do you believe that I need to get some sort of training before I start teaching online? I have been teaching for almost twenty years now and I want to break into the online industry.

You do not really have to be trained to teach online if you just want to get the job. Many colleges and organizations will accept you even if you have had no prior experience or prior training. They might ask you to take a short course on technology (i.e., how to use certain learning management system (LMS) features), but in the majority of cases this is the extent of what you will be required to take.

However, if you want to be effective online and enjoy this environment, we strongly recommend that you find a course on online pedagogy, or read books like this one and educate yourself on how to adapt your teaching style and transfer your talents online. As we mentioned throughout this book, teaching online requires a certain paradigm shift, where you start seeing your role as a teacher in a new light. Once you realize that your effectiveness depends on how you are being with your students, you will start choosing actions different from those you are accustomed to in a traditional classroom, and will focus your efforts on developing connection, engagement, and enjoyment via an interrelational climate that boosts learner autonomy while reducing isolation.

Nevertheless, no amount of training will compensate for the overall support of the institution. One cannot expect a teacher to be highly trained in all aspects of distance learning (graphic design, pedagogical design, etc.). If the institution does not see online teaching as a part of a larger system, requiring a fundamental change in your way of teaching and a certain familiarity with technology, then it will be extremely difficult for the teacher to manage this educational environment.

What should teachers who are seeking employment online be aware of?

In many cases a teacher has to fulfill numerous roles online. She is a facilitator, a resource, a guide, a negotiator, a pedagogical designer, a movie producer, a graphic artist, and a facilitator of discussions. The teacher needs to understand her different roles online and adjust her teaching practices accordingly in order to be fulfilled in this environment and so that the participants in her course can bloom. One of the main goals online is to develop learner autonomy, because learning in this environment requires high levels of independence and self-reliance. In order to support students as they struggle on their own, and foster their autonomy, the teacher needs to learn how to exercise autonomy herself. She needs to be ready to experience occasional isolation and insecurities that are caused by physical separation and delayed communication. She needs also to learn how to fight her instinct to influence her learners on an academic level, and instead hold back, providing as much emotional support as she can to the learner who is working through a learning experience adapted to him, according to his needs, in his own way. She also needs to develop her intuition and recognize signs from her students that will tell her that their connection to her is about to be broken, and use the strategies described in chapter 3 to help her learners stay within the critical in-mind boundary (CIB).

What should online students be aware of prior to applying for an online program?

Online learning is different from that in a traditional setting. The student or trainee does not have any physical interaction with his teachers or peers. At first, it might feel to him as though he is completely alone. Many learners feel isolated from other students and their teacher, but this does not need to be the case: online learning has the potential to create strong interpersonal bonds. We often build deeper relationships with our students online than with those in a traditional setting, as written communication is a powerful medium when used effectively. It is also a promising learning environment for those who are shy in class and do not like to be put "on the spot." Many introverted students blossom online and become active participants.

A feature of the online context that is at first difficult for students to understand is its seemingly faster pace. It is easy for them to become overwhelmed with work and fall behind online (much easier than in a face-to-face classroom), so it is crucial they meet their deadlines. Even if they miss one assignment, other projects can start piling up, creating more stress for them and potentially lower grades. They should print out your course calendar and post it where they can look at it daily. In addition, they should create a schedule where they designate a couple of hours every day to their online class and stick to it. If they are on top of their assignments, online learning can become more enjoyable and they will begin to see the advantages of this type of learning. They can create their own hours and study anywhere in the world. The secret is to follow their schedule and not fall behind.

Some students are intimidated by technology. They think, "I am not computer savvy. How can I succeed in a class that is fully online?" We don't want students to be afraid of technology; rather, they should understand that any new educational tool or platform requires a learning curve. It is useful for them to view tutorials prior to the beginning of the course and to log into their classroom several days before the first day of classes to see if they have any questions before class begins. If they feel lost online, they should contact their teacher immediately. Most teachers will provide their contact information, which includes their e-mail address and phone number. A teacher might choose to give out her cell number, but that is not a requirement. Make sure you know how to contact tech support in case the learning management system (LMS) does not function properly. Remember that you really cannot learn the ins and outs of technology until you actually use it. Allow yourself a couple of days to feel awkward and frustrated, but keep logging in to develop your skills. By week two, you will have mastered your LMS.

What learning strategies do you give to online students to increase their motivation and to get the most out of their program?

In the online classroom, learner autonomy is important. Each learner's autonomy will vary within the interrelational climate you construct with them, though you will see that some learners move toward independence more than others during the course. It is useful to remember that students who work on an autonomous basis with you might be more dependent in another teacher's course, and the learners who don't seem to be able to move toward autonomy with you might, with another teacher, be the most self-directed learners in the class. Learner autonomy is not a quality of the learner; it is fostered by the teacher-learner relationship. Only particular teacher-learner interrelational climates are conducive to learner autonomy, of which The Golden Climate in Distance Learning is the most effective. Some teachers are aware of this situation and may work with the learner to adapt the learning experience to the learner's individual needs and interests. If the teacher does not do this, students need to engage with the teacher, in order to make sure their interests and needs are known and taken into account in the learning process — even though it may be intimidating to approach teachers who hold a position of power. Student-teacher dialogue can strengthen their relationship, minimize the feeling of isolation common in online learners, and in turn help to prevent students withdrawing from the course.

Self-reflection and self-knowledge become crucial online. Students need to know what to do and how to be in order to get the most out of a course and do well. Even in classes with highly developed interactions, many students still feel a certain degree of isolation. This feeling is natural and can be beneficial for their learning if they can overcome it by engaging with other students and the teacher. Online learning that works is student-centered and student-driven. Students can find themselves developing the content of the class and guiding conversations with their peers — something that is usually associated with the teacher's role in the traditional classroom. While this might feel scary and strange, students are developing in their relationship with the teacher and other students their capacity to work on an autonomous basis. This means students need to develop an awareness of how best to relate to others in the class and integrate outside sources in order to create an enjoyable and rewarding learning process, and seek to create this learning climate in the way they relate to the teacher and fellow learners in each new class.

Is the Golden Climate subject or LMS specific?

No, we believe that no matter what the subject or LMS is, the main focus of an online teacher is to create with her learners an interrelational climate that fosters students' autonomy while holding them within the critical in-mind boundary. Student-teacher dialogue becomes of great importance in this context as it is the basis for developing a relationship, and structural elements of the course can be discussed and adapted to suit a student's needs and interests. This optimal learning climate is constructed differently within different student-teacher relationships. It changes constantly as students struggle to move toward autonomy and as the teacher struggles to create the space for this to happen, even as she communicates to the learner that she has him in mind.

How can you make sure some students don't dominate class discussions and that everyone participates equally?

One strategy is to make online discussion a requirement and attach an evaluation rubric to it. We discussed in detail how to develop a winning engaging activity in chapter 2. If online participation is necessary for checking progress or understanding, ensuring that every student participates online is as important as keeping some students from dominating online conversations. Therefore, it is also a good idea to limit posts to three or four for each discussion topic, and no more than two hundred words per post — or one hundred words per post in a large group — so that each student participates equally.

Another approach is to not make online participation compulsory, which might be more appropriate to avoid cluttering discussions boards when you have a large group of students. If students are working in groups while developing individual or group assignments, they are already engaging with materials, investigating areas of knowledge, constructing concepts, and exchanging ideas. You might also decide that students have the right to be shy and not participate actively in discussions. You can encourage discussion by posting thought-provoking questions or inviting people to talk about their experiences.

How can you be engaging in a synchronous classroom? I feel that my classes are lifeless and even boring. I am very engaging in my FTF classroom, but online I seem to lose my charisma.

You are not alone. It is difficult to transfer your personality online and fully engage your learners in a synchronous classroom, since you cannot see their eyes and facial expressions and there are so many other distractions to compete with. Without proper training, many teachers feel lost and become those "boring" teachers that they have always dreaded they could be. The answer to this question is a topic for another book, but here are some basic tips that will help you spice up your online presentation:

- -Make sure you incorporate suggestions from chapter 2 when developing your online presentations.
- Keep your content constantly moving so the brain always receives new impulses.
- Create slides so they are only beneficial when presented by a teacher and are not stand-alone materials.
- Remember that when you give a presentation in a virtual classroom you must use the content and technology at the same time. The way you deliver your presentation is as important for engagement as the content itself. Use your voice and intonation and pause for more emphasis;
- You can also invite another speaker and co-present a webinar. This will bring more variety to your classroom.
- Utilize features of your software, such as pointers, highlighters, and errors to direct students' attention to important information.
- We also often use various types of polling or questionnaires to break our presentation and give more control to learners.
- Frequently check students' engagement through various status tools (such as raising a hand, agreeing, etc.).

What are some don'ts in distance learning?

- Don't believe that you only create content online. First and foremost you create an experience, a climate where learning of this content becomes possible, a climate that decides student connection, engagement, enjoyment, autonomy, and performance.

- Don't assume that just because you created outstanding content it will automatically engage your learners. Constantly fight for your learners' attention and create ways to consistently measure their engagement throughout your presentation or their asynchronous work.

- Don't think that because you post regularly and write e-mails you establish connection with your students (some e-mails are not even opened and your announcements are not even read). Make sure to engage with your students on an emotional level and allow them to work on their own while periodically checking in, and actively communicate with them about their experience in the course once you feel they are getting disconnected.

- Don't assume that because your learners have mastered the technological side of distance learning, and can easily navigate your LMS and use its functions, that they know how to learn via distance. These skills require training and you are often the only source of such training for them.

- Don't think that you must be proficient in all different skills required for teaching via distance — each our for help when needed.

- Don't assume that if no questions are asked that all is understood. Provide a place where issues and concerns can be expressed in a safe way and where students can help each other.

- Don't be an instructor: tell yourself constantly that you are now a guide, resource, negotiator, and facilitator, and above all a curious, humble, and intuitive fellow traveler with each of your learners, keeping their educative well-being in mind as they move toward fulfilment in the learning process.

We hope that these few points have helped answer some of your most burning questions. If you want to contribute to this conversation, please join our online forum: www.thegoldenclimateindistancelearning.com

Conclusion

We really hope that you have enjoyed reading our book and that you have found the information presented here useful. We are certain that you will find teaching online to be a rewarding experience and that you will be effective in this educational environment. We want to leave you with just one thought. Online, one of the most important tasks of the teacher is to build a teacher-learner relationship that is conducive to autonomy. Your being a resource, guide, negotiator, and facilitator of work that takes into account the learner's needs and interests will allow the learner to live creatively and have a hand in his or her destiny, to be productive; to trust; to reach out to others — qualities that all underpin engagement, performance, and enjoyment. This way you will cultivate an optimal online relationship for teacher and learner success — the Golden Climate in Distance Learning — in which all participants in the learning community feel productive, fulfilled, and successful.

References

Benson, P. (2001). Teaching and researching autonomy in language learning. Harlow, England: Pearson Education Limited.

Berge, Z. (1999). Interaction in post-secondary Web-based learning. Educational Technology, 39(1), 5-11.

Berge, Z.L. (1995), "Facilitating Computer Conferencing: Recommendations From the Field", Educational Technology, 5 (1), 22-30.

Bolliger, D. U., & Martindale, T. (2004). Key factors influencing student satisfaction with online courses. International Journal on E-Learning, 32(1), 61-67.

Breen, M. P., & Mann, S. J. (1997). Shooting arrows at the sun: Perspectives on a pedagogy for autonomy. In P. Benson, & P. Voller, (Eds.), Autonomy and independence in language learning (pp. 132-149). London: Longman.

Burgess, J. (2006). Transactional distance theory and student satisfaction. (Doctorate dissertation, The University of West Florida). Retrieved from http://uwf.edu/vburgess/Final_Dissertation.pdf

Burnett, K. (2001). Interaction and student retention, success, and satisfaction in web-based learning. Paper presented at 67th IFLA Council and General Conference, Boston, MA.

Damasio, A. (1999). Feeling of what happens: Body and emotion in the making of consciousness. New York: Harcourt, Inc.

Daughenbaugh, R., Ensminger, D., Frederick, L., & Surry, D. (2003). Does personality type effect online versus in-class course satisfaction? The Quarterly Review of Distance Education 4(1), 65-67.

DeSantis, C. (2002). eLearners.com web site. Retrieved November 2, 2002, from http://elearners.com/

Dickinson, L. (1995). Autonomy and motivation: A literature review. System 23 (2), 165–174.

Garrison, D. R., Anderson, T., & Archer, W. (2001). Critical thinking and computer conferencing: A model and tool to assess cognitive presence. American Journal of Distance Education, 15(1), 7-23.

Gazzaniga, M.S., Russell, T., & Senior C. (2009) Methods in Mind (Cognitive Neuroscience). Cambridge: MIT Press.

Hara, N., & Kling, R. (2000). Students' distress with a Web-based distance education course: An ethnographic study of participants' experiences. Information, Communication & Society, 3, 557-579.

Herring, M., & Smaldino, S. (1997). Planning for interactive distance education: A handbook. Washington, DC: AECT Publications.

Higgins, R., Hartley, P., & Skelton, A. (2001) Getting the message across: the problem of communicating assessment feedback. Teaching in Higher Education. 6 (2), pp.269-74.

Holec, H. (1981). Autonomy in foreign language learning (first published 1979, Strasbourg: Council of Europe). Oxford: Pergamon.

Kelly, G. A. (1955). The psychology of personal constructs. New York: Norton.

Kelly, K. L., & Schorger, J. (2002). Online learning: Personalities, preferences and perceptions. (Report No. 143). (ERIC Document Reproduction Service No. ED 470 663).

Kemp, J. E. (2000). Instructional design for distance education. An interactive guidebook for designing education in the 21st century, Or, John Dewey never said it would be easy!. Bloomington, IN: Agency for Instructional Technology.

Kindred, J. (2000, May). Thinking about the online classroom: Evaluating the "ideal" versus the "real." The American Communication Journal 3(3). Retrieved November 2, 2003, from http://acjournal.org/holdings/vol3/Iss3/rogue4/kindred.html

Kostina, M. (2011). Exploration of student perceptions of autonomy, student-instructor dialogue and satisfaction in a web-based distance Russian language classroom: a mixed methods study." doctoral dissertation, University of Iowa, http://ir.uiowa.edu/etd/1003

La Ganza, W. (2001). Out of sight – not out of mind: Learner autonomy and interrelating online. Information Technology, Education and Society 2(2), 27–46.

La Ganza, W. (2004). Learner Autonomy in the Language Classroom. (Doctorate dissertation), Macquarie University, Australia.

La Ganza, W. (2008). Learner autonomy-teacher autonomy: Interrelating and the will to empower. In T. Lamb & H. Reinders (Eds.), Learner and teacher autonomy: Concepts, realities, and responses (pp. 63-79). Philadelphia: John Benjamins.

Lashbrook, J. T. (2000). Fitting in: exploring the emotional dimension of adolescent peer pressure. Adolescence, 35(140), 747–755.

Lim, C. P., & Cheah, P. T. (2003). The role of the tutor in asynchronous discussion boards: A case study of a pre-service teacher course. Education Media International. Retrieved from www.tandf.co.uk/journals/routledge/09523987.html

Little, D. (1991) Learner Autonomy: Definitions, Issues and Problems. Dublin: Authentic Language Learning Resources Limited.

Lombard, M. (2000). Presence. Phifer lecture series. Retrieved May, 2011

http://www.ccom.ua.edu:16080/News/College/102200lombard.html

Meyer, D. K., Turner, J. C., 2006. Re-conceptualizing Emotion And Motivation To Learn In Classroom Contexts. Educational Psychology Review, 18 (4), 377-390.

Moore, M. (1993). Theory of transactional distance. In D. Keegan (Ed.), Theoretical principles of distance education (pp. 22-38). London: Routledge.

Moore, M. (2007). The theory of transactional distance. In M. G. Moore (Ed.), Handbook of distance education (pp. 89-105). Mahwah, NJ: Lawrence Erlbaum Associates.

Muirhead, B. Practical Strategies for Teaching Computer-Mediated Classes. (2001). Ed Journal (15) 50, retrieved from http://www.usdla.org/html/journal/may01_Issue/article02.html.

Nielsen, J., & Pernice, K. (2010). Eyetracking Web Usability, New Riders Press.

Northrup, P. T. (2002). Online learners' preferences for interaction. The Quarterly Review of Distance Education, 3 (2), 219–226.

Ortiz, D. Oyarzun, M.P. Carretero, and N. Garay-Vitoria (2006). Virtual characters as emotional interaction element in the user interfaces. In Proceedings of AMDO. IV Conference on Articulated Motion and Deformable Objects., Andrax, Mallorca, Spain.

Panksepp, J. (1998). Affective Neuroscience: The foundations of human and animal emotions. New York: Oxford University Press.

Perreault, H., Waldman, L., Alexander, M., & Zhao, J. (2002). Overcoming barriers to successful delivery of distance-learning courses. Journal of Education for Business, 77(6), 31.

Phipps, R., & Merisotis, J. (1999). What's the Difference? A review of Contemporary Research on the Effectiveness of Distance education in Higher Education. The institute for Higher Education policy.

Prensky, M.(2001). Digital natives, digital immigrants. On the Horizon 9 (5): 1-6.

http://www.scribd.com/doc/9799/Prensky-Digital-Natives-Digital-Immigrants-Part1. Retrieved on January 28, 2009 from: http://www.webcitation.org/5eBDYI5Uw.

Revenaugh, M. (2000). Toward a 24/7 learning community. Educational Leadership, 58(2), 25-28.

Reeves, T. C. (2002). Distance education and the professorate: The issue of productivity. In C. Vrasidas and G. V. Glass (Eds.), Distance education and distributed learning (135-156). Greenwich, CT: Information Age Publishing.

Russell, Thomas L. (2001) The No Significant Difference Phenomenon: A Comparative Research Annotated Bibliography on Technology for Distance Education. IDECC, Montgomery, AL.

Saba, F. (2000). What is distance education? Defining the concepts and terms which have characterized the field. Distance-Educator. Retrieved from http://www.distance-educator.com/index1a101600.phtml.

Short, J., Williams, E., & Christie, B. (1976). The social psychology of tele-communications. London, England: John Wiley.

Simonson, M., & Russo-Converso, J. A. (2001). Managing the mandate: Role of the teacher in distance education. Paper presented at the 19th International Conference on Technology and Education, Tallahassee, FL. (ERIC Document Reproduction Service No. ED 462 979).

Smith, R. C. (2001). Group work for autonomy in Asia. The AILA Review, 15, 70–81.

Stirling, D. (1997). Toward a theory of distance education: Transactional distance. Retrieved from http://www.stirlinglaw.com/deborah/stir4.htm.

Suler, J.R. (2002). Identity management in cyberspace. Journal of Applied Psychoanalytic Studies 4, 455– 460.

Tam, M. (2000). Constructivism, Instructional Design, and Technology: Implications for Transforming Distance Learning. Educational Technology and Society, 3 (2).

Tenenbaum, S. (1961). Carl R. Rogers and non-directive teaching. In C. R. Rogers, On becoming a person: A therapist's view of psychotherapy (pp. 299–310). London: Constable.

Warschauer, M. (1998). Interaction, negotiation, and computer-mediated learning. In M. Clay (Ed.) Practical applications of educational technology in language learning. Lyon, France: National Institute of Applied Sciences.

White, C. (1999) Expectations and emergent beliefs of self-instructed language learners. System 27, 443–57. Available
www.lang.ltsn.ac.uk/resources/goodpractice.aspx?resourceid=1409

White, C. (2006). Autonomy, independence and control: Mapping the future of distance language learning. In Gardner (ed.), 56–71.

Winnicott, D. W. (1971). Playing and reality. Harmondsworth, England: Penguin.

Wood, C. (2005). Highschool.com. Edutopia, 1(4), 32-37.

Young, S. (2006). Student Views of Effective Online Teaching in Higher Education. The American Journal of Distance Education, 20(2), 65–77.

CPSIA information can be obtained at www.ICGtesting.com
Printed in the USA
LVOW130222090512

280961LV00002B/49/P